Curriculum Development for Exceptional Children

Herbert Goldstein, *Editor*

D1369679

NEW DIRECTIONS FOR EXCEPTIONAL CHILDREN
JAMES J. GALLAGHER, *Editor-in-Chief*

Number 6, June 1981

Paperback sourcebooks in
The Jossey-Bass Social and Behavioral Sciences Series

Jossey-Bass Inc., Publishers
San Francisco • Washington • London

Curriculum Development for Exceptional Children
Number 6, June 1981
    Herbert Goldstein, *Editor*

New Directions for Exceptional Children Series
James J. Gallagher, *Editor-in-Chief*

New Directions for Exceptional Children is published quarterly
by Jossey-Bass Inc., Publishers. Subscriptions, single-issue
orders, change of address notices, undelivered copies, and other
correspondence should be sent to *New Directions* Subscriptions,
Jossey-Bass Inc., Publishers, 433 California Street, San Francisco,
California 94104.

Editorial correspondence should be sent to the Editor-in-Chief,
James J. Gallagher, Frank Porter Graham Child Development Center,
University of North Carolina, Chapel Hill,
North Carolina 27514.

Library of Congress Catalogue Card Number LC 80-82569
International Standard Serial Number ISSN 0271-0625
International Standard Book Number ISBN 87589-822-X

Cover art by Willi Baum
Manufactured in the United States of America

Ordering Information

The paperback sourcebooks listed below are published quarterly and can be ordered either by subscription or single-copy.

Subscriptions cost $30.00 per year for institutions, agencies, and libraries. Individuals can subscribe at the special rate of $18.00 per year *if payment is by personal check.* (Note that the full rate of $30.00 applies if payment is by institutional check, even if the subscription is designated for an individual.) Standing orders are accepted.

Single copies are available at $6.95 when payment accompanies order, and *all single-copy orders under $25.00 must include payment.* (California, Washington, D.C., New Jersey, and New York residents please include appropriate sales tax.) For billed orders, cost per copy is $6.95 plus postage and handling. (Prices subject to change without notice.)

To ensure correct and prompt delivery, all orders must give either the *name of an individual* or an *official purchase order number.* Please submit your order as follows:

Subscriptions: specify series and subscription year.
Single Copies: specify sourcebook code and issue number (such as, IR8).

Mail orders for United States and Possessions, Latin America, Canada, Japan, Australia, and New Zealand to:
Jossey-Bass Inc., Publishers
433 California Street
San Francisco, California 94104

Mail orders for all other parts of the world to:
Jossey-Bass Limited
28 Banner Street
London EC1Y 8QE

New Directions for Exceptional Children Series
James J. Gallagher, *Editor-in-Chief*

EC1   *Ecology of Exceptional Children,* James J. Gallagher
EC2   *Language Intervention with Children,* Diane Bricker
EC3   *Young Exceptional Children,* James J. Gallagher
EC4   *Parents and Families of Handicapped Children,* James J. Gallagher
EC5   *Socioemotional Development,* Nicholas J. Anastasiow

JAN 4 1981

Contents

Editor's Notes

Educational programs for the mentally retarded in Western societies can be traced back almost two centuries. Theories of human physiology and optimism that mentally retarded individuals were amenable to treatment suggested that substantive and progressive growth in these programs was possible.

Although efforts were made to determine what retarded individuals needed to learn in order to function in society, this interest in curriculum was displaced by questions concerning the etiology of mental retardation, and studies of the learning characteristics of retarded students. Curriculum issues thus became the province of educators. The rapid proliferation of educational programs drew attention to administrative and logistical problems, leaving the design and implementation of curriculum to teachers. Thus, curriculum development quickly became a cottage industry.

Recognizing that curriculums unique to each classroom deprived mentally retarded students of continuity and breadth in educational experiences, a number of school districts initiated curriculum committees to develop curriculum guides. In theory, at least, these guides were to form a common frame of reference for the district's special education program. Despite a consensus that curriculum guides were of relatively little help in unifying programs, the momentum carried this practice well into the 1960s and, in fact, continues in some districts today.

In the mid 1960s, a more objective approach to curriculum development was proposed by a small number of subject matter specialists. Supported by the then Bureau for the Education of the Handicapped, U.S. Office of Education, the work began. This issue of New Directions for Exceptional Children is a graphic representation of the development technology evolved by these projects with the chapters each representing an operational unit. The initial and ongoing process of collecting background information is presented in the chapter by Herbert Goldstein. Warren Heiss describes how development groups (curriculum writers) organize content into teachable formats. In the chapter by Marjorie Goldstein, the projects' link with the reality of the classroom is set forth as a model adopted by most

1

projects. Ray Bepko deals with the complexities of collecting evaluation data from teachers for the purpose of curriculum revision as a prelude to general dissemination. James Budde combines the elements of project operations into a systems construct for management purposes. And Leon Smith and Sandra Greenberg discuss a research project that typifies issues emerging in the course of the development effort.

Herbert Goldstein
Editor

Herbert Goldstein is professor of educational psychology in the Department of Educational Psychology, Program in Special Education, New York University.

The unfolding of curriculum for the mentally retarded has been variable in the nature and scope of content. While many factors contributed to change, the most powerful appears to be educators' view of the role of mature mentally retarded persons in society.

Conceptual and Structural Foundations of Curriculum

Herbert Goldstein

Unlike regular education, education of the mentally retarded does not have a long history of formalized curriculum development. Education of the mentally retarded originated with the medical profession early in the nineteenth century (Itard, 1932). Physicians dominated this aspect of education in either pedagogic or administrative roles for the better part of a century. During this period, educational programs were the province of public institutions for the mentally retarded (Fernald, 1893; Rogers, 1888).

Early in the twentieth century, primary responsibility for education began to pass from the public institution to the public school. This century saw the ascendency first of psychology and then of special education as a result of the rise of the mental test movement (Nowery, 1945) and the establishment of public school provisions for the mentally retarded (Wallin, 1955).

Itard's Experiment

In 1799, an adolescent boy was taken from the forests of the department of Averyron in France. The boy, Victor, was described as

H. Goldstein (Ed.). *New Directions for Exceptional Children: Curriculum Development for Exceptional Children*, no. 6. San Francisco: Jossey-Bass, June 1981

4

savage, animal-like, and without language. Under ordinary circumstances, this child, like the ten recorded feral children captured before him, would have become a curiosity for public display. The status of knowledge and the philosophic climate of France, however, dictated that habilitative action was to be taken in his case.

At this time, the theories of Étienne Bonnet, the Abbé de Condillac (1930), and Jean-Jacques Rousseau (1896) had captured the interest of scientists and educators alike. Condillac's theory accounted for the acquisition of knowledge through the experiences of the individual and placed particular emphasis on the senses as avenues for learning. Rousseau emphasized the relationship between the experiences and the developmental patterns of an individual (Boyd, 1911). He contended that the extent to which they were related determined the extent to which the full potential of the individual would be reached. As sensationalists, Condillac and Rousseau subscribed to Locke's position that the child was born a blank tablet, upon which perceptions of the outside world were imprinted through experience (Locke, n.d.).

Jean-Marc Gaspard Itard (1932) was a young physician employed in a school for the deaf in France. Itard was completely taken by the theory of sensationalism and one of its strong advocates. He volunteered to take responsibility for the training of the wild boy, despite the fact that two prior attempts to train him had met with failure (Seguin, 1907).

Itard's first program for the boy was psychologically oriented, to conform with the theories of Condillac and Rousseau. His five-point plan was to make social life attractive and thereby counteract the boy's tendency toward solitude; to sensitize his nervous system through energetic stimulation of the senses and through emotionally loaded situations; to introduce and broaden concepts both in terms of material objects and interpersonal relationships; to stimulate speech through auditory training and imitation; and to increase intelligence by having the boy live through certain experiences associated with his needs, thus acquiring the ideas requisite for generalization.

Itard instituted this program in 1801 and followed it for a year. The results obtained did not approach his expectations. In the following year, Itard changed his program from a predominantly psychological frame of reference to an almost purely physiological frame of reference. This new three-point program was designed to develop sensory perception, intelligence, and emotional stability.

In 1805, Itard discontinued his efforts to habilitate the Wild Boy of Aveyron and sent him to the institution at Bicêtre. Sometime later, the boy was entrusted to the matron who had cared for him during his stay with Itard. Victor remained with this woman until his death in 1828. During these years, he showed no further improvement.

While Itard considered the undertaking to have been less than successful, the French Academy decorated him and acknowledged his contribution to education. It is difficult to determine the extent to which education might have profited had Itard set more realistic aspirations for his methods. As it was, the reorganization and refinement of his principles of education were left to his student, Edward Seguin (Seguin, 1841).

Seguin and the Physiological Method

With the encouragement of Itard, Edward Seguin devoted himself to the study and treatment of idiocy. Through observation of Itard's work and experimentation with his own methods, he was able to work out the basic principles of a system of physiological education (Holman, 1914).

Seguin's view of his work was much broader than Itard's. While he approached the education of the mentally retarded in the same scientific spirit, his goals were considerably more humanistic. In keeping with his subscription to the doctrine of Saint-Simonism (Booth, 1871), he viewed education as a means for the betterment of all classes of people.

Seguin's first attempt to educate a mentally retarded boy using the physiological method was generally judged to be successful and encouraged him to institute a school for mentally retarded children. In 1839, a commission of the Parisian Academy of Sciences examined his students and concluded that, "he had undoubtedy solved the problem of idiot education" (Boyd, 1914, p. 92).

Seguin's curriculum was based on the assumption that "Idiocy is a specific infirmity of the craniospinal axis, produced by deficiency of nutrition in utero and in neonati" (1841, p. 29). He conceived of two types of defect in the nervous system: those in the central nervous system and those in the peripheral nervous system. Of the two, those in the central nervous system were considered the more limiting. In his view, physiological education should not be confined only to academic and motor learning of the child; the progress in learning from gross motor activities through abstract generalization was expected to eventuate in hygienic and moral learning. He planned to achieve these results by opening the defective avenues from the faulty peripheral receptors to the brain by muscle and sense training. Where the central nervous system was defective, training would bombard the cells and stimulate increased cortical function.

Seguin's system of education progressed through three stages: motor education, sensory education, and intellectual and moral education.

Motor Education. This stage of education began with exercise of purposeful immobility where the child learned to sit, stand, and recline of his own will, and then progressed to motility. Exercises and equipment were designed to promote coordination and strength. In all cases, the progression in learning was from large muscle activities to small.

Sensory Education. Once motor and coordination problems were well on the way to correction, training of the senses began. Considerable emphasis was placed on the development of accuracy of the hands. According to Seguin, "The hand is the organ of prehension. Its incapacity puts a barrier between the idiot and everything to be acquired" (1841, p. 77). By *prehension* Seguin meant the complex actions involved in grasping—taking, holding, and relinquishing. In this phase, exercises were designed to enhance skills in each activity. Thus, the training of the hand proceeded in the direction of increasingly complex activities involving smaller muscles of the hand and resulting finally in the development of tactile skills. Training of taste and smell followed the training of hand coordination and touch. Training of audition and vision followed.

Seguin started by presenting music, because of it stimulatory powers. Music was selected first to fit the mood of physical activities, then to sensitize the child to such basics as vibrations and tone qualities. Next, it was blended into speech. Finally, it was intermingled in the exercises and habits of the children as a healthy stimulus. Efforts to expand speech ability continued from this point on.

Sight training was also started on a simple level. Objects long familiar to the child were displaced or removed. Intensity of light in the room was controlled and varied. Color and shape discrimination became the basis for a lengthy series of exercises aimed at developing sensitivity. Judgment and estimating were other skills to be acquired.

Throughout the training in vision, Seguin pressed for eye-hand co-ordination.

After the child had mastered these skills, he or she was ready for exercises leading to skills in drawing, writing, and reading. In all cases, the goal included not only the motor skills involved in the task but also comprehension of the material being produced or read. It is of some interest that Seguin found it very difficult to fit prepared reading materials to the levels required by his pupils.

Intellectual and Moral Education. The acquisition of reading and language skills introduced a new phase of education. Identification of the physical properties of objects permitted working toward skills in classification and the higher-order abstractions associated with them.

Seguin's contributions received considerable acclaim (Davies, 1930). He has been credited with devising a curriculum and method for the instruction of mentally retarded children and for lending his energies to the establishment and organization of state schools for the mentally retarded in the United States. His methods were popular for many years and saw considerable use in American schools and institutions.

Seguin made a third contribution that in its particular area, ranks with the others: He applied principles of learning to the education of mentally retarded children. Inductive learning was one of the major strategies in Sequin's system. By structuring the learning situation so that the child had to acquire the concept inherent in the lesson, Seguin enhanced the probability of generalization. Inductive learning in the first two areas of his curriculum, motor and sensory education, made possible the acquisition of the abstractions basic to his third area, hygienic and moral education.

Long before reinforcement became an area for experimentation and a common term, Seguin integrated it into his program. As he wrote, "Caresses are of great power for good or evil and must be reserved as rewards and stimuli" (1841, p. 150).

It can be seen that Seguin had proposed a solution to two major problems in the education of mentally retarded children: what to do and how to do it. Unfortunately, educators seized only upon his prescription for what to do. This was noted by Dr. Maria Montessori at the close of the nineteenth century while observing classes for mentally retarded children at the Bicêtre. She wrote, "I saw that it was the didactic apparatus of Seguin far more than his method which was

being used, although the French text was in the hands of educators"
(Montessori, 1912, p. 36).

The Montessori Method

Maria Montessori was an Italian physician who had psychiatric
training. In the course of her duties as assistant doctor in the
psychiatric clinic of the University of Rome, she became interested in
the mentally retarded children housed in the hospitals for the mentally
ill. Her interest in these children led her to Seguin's texts. Montessori
read Seguin's work and came to the conclusion that, while his
methods had value, his rationale for a predominantly medical approach to education for mentally deficient children was specious
(Montessori, 1912).

Montessori studied Seguin's methods and traveled through
Europe to observe them in use. Her work led to the development of
the State Orthophrenic School for mentally retarded children. Children were from public schools. Later, mentally retarded children from
hospitals for the mentally ill were admitted to this school.

Montessori directed the school from 1898 to 1900 and trained
teachers of mentally retarded children in her methods. A major
portion of her time, however, was spent working directly with the
children. Her results led her to believe that her methods were far
more effective than those being used in most schools.

In the course of her work with mentally retarded children,
Montessori developed a great variety of didactic materials. She observed teachers using these materials and came to the conclusion that
didactic materials alone were not enough; the teacher's personality
must become part of the pedagogic picture if positive results were to
be obtained.

Montessori taught a number of her mentally retarded pupils to
read and write sufficiently well to pass regular school examinations.
She attributed this feat to her method of instruction, which, according
to her, so enhanced their psychological adjustment that they could
work at peak efficiency. The methods then being used with nonhandicapped children, she felt, acted to inhibit learning. From her results,
she concluded that nonhandicapped children would profit from her
methods. Subsequently, she devoted much of her writing to educational practices relevant to the development of nonhandicapped
children.

Montessori's method was criticized by Kilpatrick (1914) and by Morgan (1913), mainly in terms of its application with normal children. As Kirk and Johnson state it, "The greatest defect in her theory is the assumption that there is a transfer of training from didactic materials to life situations" (1951, p. 81).

Nevertheless, Montessori's insistence that the education of mentally retarded children was a pedagogic and not a medical problem strengthened education as a force in dealing with mental retardation. It is difficult to ascertain the extent of her influence on this movement. The literature, however, shows an increasing ascendancy of educators after her arrival on the scene.

Decroly

The early twentieth century saw a rapid expansion of educational programs for mentally retarded children. One of the most noteworthy programs was that of Ovide Decroly, a Belgian physician. Decroly, a contemporary of Montessori, endorsed Montessori's thesis that the education of mentally deficient children was predominantly the province of educators (Hamaide, 1924).

Decroly based his system of education on the proposition that the school must be in close contact with life in order to teach effectively; the child's interests and needs should be basic to the lesson. He therefore devised a program based on the child's need to play that, under the guise of games, introduced a sequence of new learnings.

Like Montessori, Decroly left special education in order to apply his methods with nonhandicapped children. It remained for his student Descoeudres (1928) to elaborate upon his work. This she did, in considerable detail, as she carried out a program of instruction in the public schools of Belgium.

The Development of Curriculums for Special Classes

From the beginning, the curriculums and methods of instruction in public school classes for the mentally retraded reflected the influence of sensationalism. Seguin's method, long the property of institutional schools, diffused to the public schools in the form of sense training basic to reading and writing, plus manual training in basketry, woodworking, and the like (Esten, 1900). The spread of the

Seguin method to the public schools owed much to the fact that the schools drew a good number of teachers from the public institutions (Steinback, 1918). Teacher training for special classes was at first the province of institutions for the mentally retarded and only later of universities and colleges (Johnstone, 1914).

In a comparatively short time, the notion of the school as the site of intrinsic learning began to be supplanted by the idea of the school as an influence on social adjustment. To some degree, this concept was crystallized by the work of Binet (1914), Norsworthy (1906), and Witmer (1911), who demonstrated that mentally retarded individuals differed from nonhandicapped persons not in kind but in degree. The implication of this concept for education was clearly stated by Hollingworth, who wrote "The fact that the feebleminded are different from average children not in kind but in degree only is of fundamental importance for education; for it follows that no mysterious or unique matter or method is necessarily required in the task of training them. They can learn the same things that other children learn, up to the limits of their capacity. We need not look about for unique 'physiological methods,' 'linguistic methods,' or 'medico-pedagogical methods,' nor may we hope for any special results from them. The feebleminded differ from ordinary children only in amount of ability, not in the kind of abilities which they possess." (1922, pp. 90–91).

The Modified Institutional Curriculum

The curriculum proposed by Anderson (1917) was the first systematic program for special classes for mentally retarded children in the public schools. Anderson's curriculum, an adaptation of a then popular institutional program for mildly mentally retarded persons, proposed to replace implementation of the traditional public school curriculum in special classes. Her program stressed manual and industrial training, and she suggested that the course of study for mentally retarded children should include habits of personal cleanliness, sense training, manual training, vocational and industrial training, gardening, academic work, and speech training, insofar as it was found to be worthwhile. A major portion of the curriculum was devoted to activities designed to train the child in manual and vocational skills.

The Anderson curriculum proposed to organize classes for the retarded on three levels: the kindergarten, for children with a mental age ranging from two to four years; the departmental division, for children with a mental age between five and nine; and vocational classes, for children and youths with a mental age above nine.

The departmental division derived its title from the design of the curriculum for this level, which divided into five areas, with one teacher responsible for each: physical training; household skills, with emphasis on kitchen work; shop training; manual training; and academic work. At this level, specific vocational training was not the goal. Instead, the purpose, as Anderson wrote, was "training the mind of the defective through his hands" (1917, p. 214).

The curriculum for the vocational classes occupied the final years of the child's schooling. It was designed to train the children for specific jobs. Skills in rug making, furniture repairing, chair caning, cobbling, boot blacking, and other blind alley positions were emphasized in boy's classes. Girls learned how to be servants and houseworkers; how to knit, crochet, and sew; and how to make hats, rugs, and boxes.

Continuity in this curriculum was provided by the concept that early manual and physical training in the kindergarten and departmental division resulted in more precise and speedy manual work in the vocational training phase.

The strengths and weaknesses of Anderson's formulation are combined in its main characteristic, oversimplicity. For the most part, this curriculum places the problems of education in a one-to-one relationship with the solutions. To Anderson's credit, however, it must be recognized that for the first time, this curriculum gave the school a clear and concise method for meeting its stated goals. The fact that both goals and methods were oversimplified is consistent with the early position of this curriculum in the developmental progression of curriculum building.

Anderson's curriculum was based on then popular notions of the characteristics and learning abilities of mentally retarded persons as well as the requisites for social adjustment. Its premise was that the major avenue of learning for mentally retarded persons is handwork and repetitive physical acts. With respect to social adjustment, the curriculum presupposed that, once a person is given a remunerative position, all else will follow.

Curriculums developed after Anderson's tended both to stress a broader concept of the goals of public education and to display a greater understanding of the concept of individual differences. Subsequent educators and psychologists tended to discuss the goals and function of the school in terms more general than Anderson's. In contrast to Anderson's direct occupational prescription, Woodrow stated that "a rough and tentative estimate can be made of the sort of life work which the child may ultimately make his own" (1923, p. 260). Of the nature of the curriculum, Hollingworth (1922) wrote that it was "a matter that must be decided on the basis of social aims" (1922, p. 92). To differentiate social aims, Wallin suggested, "We should go out into the community and find out what the community wants" (1924, p. 171).

With such changes in the conceptualization of education of the mentally retarded, statements of the goals of the school eventuated in generalizations. According to Odell, "Those in charge should have very definitely in mind as an aim the preparation of pupils of inferior mentality to become as satisfactory members of the community as possible" (1931, p. 34). Inskeep wrote, "For them, as for normal children, it is the same goal by which, consciously or unconsciously, every school system in a democracy is measured—the training of self-controlled, self-supporting citizens" (1926, p. 2).

Whipple (1927) did not state her conception of the goals of the school explicitly, but they are evident from her criteria for the selection of subject matter to be taught, and they are essentially in agreement with the goals stated by others. Davis was more specific: "The general aim or objective of special school training [for mentally retarded children] is to make of the individuals directly concerned in our study law-abiding members of the community in which they may live, socially adaptable, and economically self-sufficient, capable of complete or at least partial self-support through worthwhile labor and productivity" (1927, p. 16).

At this stage in curriculum development, formulations of the goals of education shifted from broad generalizations to more definitive statements. This trend may have been hastened by the conclusions of the White House Conference on Child Health and Protection (1931), which recognized that the lack of clarity about the purpose and objectives of the education of mentally retarded children had vitiated the efforts of the schools and minimized the desirable results.

Curriculum developers began to spell out goals in more specific terms. Hungerford, Deprospo, and Rosenzweig (1952), Ingram (1935, 1953), Kirk and Johnson (1951), and Martens (1950) were basically in agreement with the broad goals of public education as stated by the Educational Policies Commission of the National Education Association (1946), which distinguished goals pertinent to the education of mentally retarded, average, and superior children. Each writer delineated the implications of these goals for mentally retarded children; in all cases, the goals implied adequate personal, social, and occupational adjustment.

Early Problems in Curriculum Building and Organization

The statement and clarification of goals for the education of mentally retarded children introduced the two problems inherent in building and implementing a curriculum to meet the stated goals: selection of pertinent subject matter and activities and organization of variations in emphasis on areas of subject matter and activities.

Selection of Subject Matter and Activities. A perusal of the literature on curriculum for the education of mentally retarded children shows that selection and organization of the areas of learning has proceeded from the simple to the complex. In the first stages, curriculum development was devoted, for the most part, to differentiating content. In a comparatively short time, however, consensus was reached on this aspect of the problem, and attention turned to the organization of subject matter and activities. This second phase has not yet and may never be entirely resolved, since it reflects the curriculm builder's conception of how to meet the goals of education.

Attention to the problem of selecting the subject matter and activities for the curriculum increased following the formulation proposed by Anderson. Guiding principles for selection of subject matter and activities were proposed. Woodrow (1923), Odell (1931), Horn (1924), and Martens (1938) advocated a curriculum that emphasized personal and social competence along with literacy skills. Others, notably Wallin (1924), Whipple (1927), and Inskeep (1926), recommended that the regular school curriculum should be the focus but that it should be modified to accommodate the learning problems of retarded students. The concept of the watered-down curriculum has been credited to Inskeep, who contended that the regular class curriculum had only to be truncated, simplified, and stretched over the conventional school years.

Ingram's (1935) suggestions for subject matter and activities represent an extension beyond the limits of the regular school curriculum. She suggested the following as curriculum content:

health, tool subjects, group and community life, family life, leisure, and vocations. To a considerable degree, curriculums devised since Ingram (Hungerford, DeProspo, and Rosenzweig, 1952; Kirk and Johnson, 1951) adopt a very similar content structure.

Organization of Subject Matter. While there was some disagreement about specific aspects of the content of curriculum for the mentally retarded, there was total agreement about how this curriculum should be implemented: children should confront content in as real and lifelike a situation as could be structured.

Organization of subject matter into practical experiences has its roots in the project method of teaching capably set forth by Stevenson (1921). This system of organization focuses on the day-to-day problems that emerge from the experiences of the children and marshals the skills required for the solution of problems into a comprehensive plan. This type of organization implies that activities and materials used in solving a problem must be true to life; the problem-solving situation must be structured to emphasize reasoning rather than memorization; solving the problem should summate in principles basic to future generalization, not in simple manipulations or techniques; and the act of solving the problem must come to a successful conclusion (Stevenson, 1921).

Davis (1927), Inskeep (1926), Martens (1950), and Wallin (1955) are among those who have recommended the project or unit system as a matrix for learning. It remained for Ingram, however, to organize areas of learning into a comprehensive system of units by maturational levels. Ingram (1935) suggests six criteria for the selection of units: the unit should grow out of real-life situations; the unit should be suited to the child's social, physical, and mental level of development; the unit should further both individual and group growth; the unit should provide for the development of desirable habits and attitudes of social living as well as for the acquisition of appropriate knowledge and skills; the unit should be developed so that the interests, skills, habits, and attitudes fostered by it carry over into life outside of school; and the unit should provide for practical use of the tool subjects.

Ingram (1935) suggested that all units should offer children three types of experience: contact with real things; vicarious experiences through pictures, models, and so on; and expressive experiences, with opportunities to verbalize and act out the results of prior experiences.

While the unit receives the major emphasis in Ingram's curriculum, academic areas are not entirely overlooked. In addition to the areas of academic learning encompassed by the unit, Ingram schedules blocks of class time for the acquisition of skills in the tool subjects.

In application, however, teachers were far more attracted to the formula for organizing the unit of instruction than to the prescriptions for the content of instruction. The concept of curriculum as a developmentally organized array of content, a concept promulgated by Ingram and her predecessors, was abandoned in favor of such teacher-designated "topics" as the supermarket, healthful diet, and the use of public transportation. Within the context of the unit, the teacher attempted to include concepts and facts at the students' functioning levels with academic subject matter. For example, in the supermarket unit arithmetic might include simulated purchasing. Reading of advertisements and product labels might accommodate language arts, with science, art, and music similarly incorporated.

In a short time, the process of curriculum development became a classroom enterprise, and each teacher assumed the responsibility of selecting and assembling the total program for the class. This acted to isolate teachers from one another operationally. It soon became evident that local district programs were significantly discontinuous. There was very little concordance in either the content of instruction or the emphasis on subject matter.

To counteract such discontinuity, local districts and some state education agencies formed curriculum committees to construct curriculum guides that could be used by all teachers in the special education program as a common basis for selecting and organizing units. The curriculum guide movement became international in scope, and the concept of the teacher as curriculum specialist gained prominence. The interpolation of educational goals and objectives has remained vested in teachers since the mid 1950s, however, with concomitant discontinuity in local programs (Simches and Bohn, 1963).

The abandonment of comprehensive efforts in curriculum development was not universally condoned. Meyen (1969) attempted to counteract discontinuity by introducing a master teacher into local districts. The master teacher was a member of the local special education teaching staff who had been trained to guide teachers in coordinated use of the curriculum guide. While Meyen's project demonstrated the effectiveness of this approach, it, like many innovations, did not diffuse beyond the limits of his project. Later, he devised a plan to bolster structure and systematic implementation of teaching units (Meyen, 1972). Goldstein, Minskoff, and Mischio (1969) found in their study of teachers' use of a curriculum guide that less than one third of the teachers used the guide in accordance with the criteria established by the developers. These results were based on one year of training for teachers in implementation of the guide and two years of follow-up training and consultation. Despite these findings, the curriculum guide continues to be the foundation of educational content.

At about the same time, studies of the mentally retarded in society were being pursued in universities and research centers (Clarke and Clarke, 1972; Goldstein, 1964; Windle, 1962). With remarkable unanimity, these studies showed that the social adaptive problems of a disproportionate number of mentally retarded individuals could be traced to inadequate sociopersonal skills. This lent credibility to the theories stated earlier by Seguin, Montessori, Decroly, and others and once again drew the school into focus as a force in the social growth and development of the mentally retarded.

Hungerford, DeProspo, and Rosenzweig (1952) responded to the results of follow-up studies of mentally retarded school leavers in the New York City school system by developing a curriculum that emphasized social and vocational learning. Years ahead of its time, this curriculum provided formalized instruction from school-entering age onward. The curriculum, Occupational Education, became the core around which all other content areas were centered.

In contrast to curriculum guides, comprehensive lesson plans were prepared by a central development group and distributed to teachers for implementation. By the middle of their school career, students were ready to study a range of occupational issues, including related knowledge about using one's income, leisure time, and the like. During the later school years, the focus was on getting and keeping a job.

While this core curriculum, as it came to be known, became the foundation for the education of mildly retarded students in New York City schools, it was ignored by most other school systems. Approbation and endorsement by leading educators and administrators did little to counteract the unfounded conviction that curriculum needs to be indigenous to each community. This conviction, identified by Berman and McLaughlin (1975) as the "not invented here" syndrome, persists to the present in many communities and dramatically impedes the innovation process in special education.

The trend toward homemade curriculums was interrupted in the late 1960s when the Bureau for the Education of the Handicapped (BEH) in the U.S. Office of Education underwrote a number of projects for the mentally retarded, including the Social Learning Curriculum, Project Math, Project MORE, I CAN, and Biological Sciences Curriculum Study. These curriculums are described or referred to in the chapters by Heiss, Bepko, and M. Goldstein. As these authors demonstrate, the contribution of these projects to special education transcends the simple selection and organization of the content of instruction. They have also evolved technologies for developing curriculum that go well beyond the conventional procedures used by curriculum committees.

Because of the increasing costs of education for the handicapped, it is unlikely that large curriculum development efforts on the scale of those discussed in this sourcebook will find the necessary support in the future. It seems likely that more modest endeavors will evolve on a more restricted geographical basis, locally or regionally. Motivation for continued efforts in curriculum development will likely include pressure for curriculum reform and clarification from the minimum competency test movement.

Curriculum in the 1980s. With the advent of P.L. 94-142, The Education of All Handicapped Children Act of 1975, compliance with mandates became a preoccupation at all educational levels. Once again, the focus was on the form of education, to the virtual exclusion of substance. There are indications, however, that a more balanced approach to special education is a not too distant prospect. The source of change appears to be rooted in the basic competency test movement. In thirty-six states, passing a basic competency test is a prerequisite for award of a high school diploma (Jaeger and Tittle, 1980). The notable failure of the vast majority of mentally retarded students to pass basic competency tests has led many states to exempting these students from taking the test (Rosewater, 1979). Apart from the other issues that this practice raises, McClung (1978) and others contend that this exemption is in violation of the Fourteenth Amendment of the U.S. Constitution. Equally important is the matter of curricular validity. It has been argued that basic competency tests do not reflect the learning experiences of mentally retarded students

(Rosewater, 1979). To counter this charge, it has been recommended that successful fulfillment of the Individualized Education Program (IEP) required by P.L. 94-142 should be accepted as the equivalent of passing the statewide basic competency test (*Northport-East Northport Union Free School District* v. *New York State Department of Education*, 1980). In this lawsuit, the court did not address the question of the IEP as a substitute for curriculum. Instead, the decision was based on a due process issue: handicapped students were not provided with time to prepare for the exams.

In time, such issues as due process and the validity and reliability of competency tests will probably be settled in ways satisfactory to all parties. The matter of curriculum for the mentally retarded represents a more pressing challenge for special educators. This challenge can only be met through the evolution of comprehensive curriculums that are consistent with the goals of education and relevant to the growth and development of mentally retarded students. Only in this way can local education agencies begin to respond to the need for program continuity for students and to the scrutiny to which the IEP will be subjected if it is accepted for retarded students in lieu of passing a state basic competency test.

Summary

Although curriculum for the retarded emerged well after curriculum for regular education, it had an auspicious beginning. Itard and, later, Seguin combined social philosophy and learning theory to evolve an educational program notable for its creativity, thoroughness, and internal consistency. Seguin, in particular, articulated a physiological explanation for mental retardation and designed curriculum for instruction to remedy the condition. While advances in medical knowledge showed his explanation to be in error, his curriculum and the principles of learning incorporated in it have, for the most part, retained credibility to the present time.

In the century after Itard attempted to improve the antisocial behavior of a feral child, there was a slow but continuing change from a predominantly medical approach to the education of retarded children to a psychoeducational approach. The goals of education for retarded children reflected the prevailing expectations for the role of the mature retarded in society.

As the responsibility of public education for mentally retarded students increased, teachers became the most active single group of specialists on the curriculum front. With rare exceptions, it was left to them to select or design curriculum for their classes. As a result, formulas for organizing curriculum were developed to help teachers to achieve consistency in their work with mentally retarded students.

What proved to be the most popular formula was designed by Ingram in the early 1930s. After prescribing the content elements for curriculum, she recommended the content to be organized into units of instruction. For a number of reasons, special educators focused on form rather than substance and devoted much of their attention and energies to the design of a foolproof format for the preparation of units. As a result, the balanced curriculum gave way to a predominantly academic program augmented by random prosocially oriented units. The Occupational Education Curriculum developed in New York City by Hungerford and his associates represented a powerful reestablishment of the balanced curriculum, but it went largely ignored elsewhere.

After a hiatus of some fifteen years, a number of curriculum development efforts emerged with the support of the Bureau for the Education of the Handicapped, U.S. Office of Education. While these efforts represent a wide array of content areas, they all share a prosocial orientation, which restores the balance of otherwise academic programs. As with other innovations in education, it seems likely that adoption of these curriculums will be a slow process.

Looking ahead into the 1980s at the influence of P.L. 94-142 and the competency test movement, it can be predicted that the role of curriculum will become better defined since it provides a means for structuring the education of the mentally retarded to conform with legislation and adjudicated mandates.

References

Anderson, M. *Education of Defectives in the Public School.* New York: World, 1917.

Berman, P., and McLauglin, M. W. *Federal Programs Supporting Educational Change. Vol. IV: The Findings in Review.* Santa Monica, Calif.: Rand, 1975.

Binet, A., and Simon, T. *Mentally Defective Children.* (M. Drummond, Trans.) New York: Longman, 1914.

Board of Education Northport-East Northport Union Free School District v. *Gordon Ambach, Commissioner of Education of the State of New York,* State of New York Supreme Court, Albany, 1980.

Booth, A. J. *Saint Simon and Saint-Simonism.* London: Longman, 1871.

Boyd, W. *From Locke to Montessori.* London: Harrap, 1914.

Clarke, A. M., and Clarke, A. D. B. "Problems of Employment and Occupation of the Mentally Subnormal." In M. Adams, (Ed.), *The Mentally Subnormal: The Social Casework Approach.* London: Heinemann, 1972.

Condillac, Abbé de. *Condillac's Treatise on the Sensations.* (G. Carr, Trans.) Los Angeles: University of Southern California, 1930.

Davis, G. P. *What Shall the Public School Do for the Feebleminded?* Cambridge, Mass.: Harvard University Press, 1927.

Davies, S. P. *Social Control of the Mentally Deficient.* New York: Crowell, 1930.

Descoeudres, A. *Education of Mentally Defective Children.* (E. F. Row, Trans.) Boston: Heath, 1928.

DeYoung, C. A. *Introduction to American Public Education.* New York: McGraw-Hill, 1955.

Educational Policies Commission. *Policies for Education in American Democracy.* Washington, D.C.: National Education Association, 1946.

Esten, R. A. "Backward Children in the Public Schools." *Journal of Psychoasthenics,* September, 1900, p. 2.

Fernald, W. E. "History of Treatment of the Feebleminded." In I. C. Barrows (Ed.), *Proceedings of National Conference of Charities and Correction.* Boston: Ellis, 1893.

Fort, S. J. "Special Schools for Special Children." *Journal of Psychoasthenics,* September, 1900, p. 31.

Goldstein, H. "Social and Occupational Adjustment." In H. R. Stevens and R. Heber (Eds.), *Mental Retardation: A Review of Research.* Chicago: University of Chicago Press, 1964.

Goldstein, H., Minskoff, E., and Mischio, G. S. *A Demonstration-Research Project in Curriculum and Methods of Instruction for Elementary-Level Mentally Retarded Children.* Washington, D.C.: Bureau of Education for the Handicapped, U.S. Office of Education, 1969.

Hamaide, A. *The Decroly Class.* (J. L. Hunt, Trans.) New York: Dutton, 1924.

Hollingworth, L. *The Psychology of Subnormal Children.* New York: Macmillan, 1922.

Holman, M. *Seguin and His Physiological Method of Education.* London: Pittman, 1914.

Horn, J. L. *Education of Exceptional Children.* New York: Century, 1924.

Hungerford, R. H., DeProspo, C. J., and Rosenzweig, L. E. "Education of the Mentally Handicapped in Childhood and Adolescence." *American Journal of Mental Deficiency,* October 1957, 214–228.

Ingram, C. P. *Education of the Slow-Learning Child.* New York: World, 1935.

Ingram, C. P. *Education of the Slow-Learning Child.* New York: Ronald Press, 1953.

Inskeep, A. D. *Teaching Dull and Retarded Children.* New York: Macmillan, 1926.

Itard, J. M. G. *The Wild Boy of Aveyron.* (G. and M. Humphrey, Trans.) New York: Century, 1932.

Jaeger, R. M., and Tittle, C. K. (Eds.). *Minimum Competency Achievement Testing: Motives, Models, and Consequences.* Berkeley, Calif.: McCutchan, 1980.

Johnstone, E. R. "The Extension of the Care of the Feebleminded." *Journal of Psychoasthenics,* September 1914, p. 4.

Kilpatrick, W. H. *The Montessori System Examined.* Boston: Houghton Mifflin, 1914.

Kirk, S.A., and Johnson, G. O. *Educating the Retarded Child.* New York: Houghton Mifflin, 1951.

Locke, J. *An Essay on Human Understanding.* London: George Routledge & Sons, n.d.

McClung, M. "Are Competency Testing Programs Fair? Legal?" *Phi Delta Kappan,* 1978, 59 (6), 397–400.

Martens, E. H. "Home Economics for the Handicapped Pupil." *Practical Home Economics,* 1938, 16, 338–340.

Martens, E. H. "Curriculum Adjustments for the Mentally Retarded." Washington, D.C.: Federal Security Agency, *Office of Education Bulletin,* 1950, no. 2.

Meyen, E. L. "Preparation of Life Experience Units for Teaching the Educable Mentally Retarded." In E. L. Meyen, G. Vergason, and R. J. Whelan (Eds.), *Strategies for Teaching Exceptional Children.* Denver: Love, 1972.

Meyen, E. L. *Demonstration of Dissemination Practices on Special Class Instruction for the Mentally Retarded: Utilizing Master Teachers as In-Service Educators—Final Report.* Washington, D.C.: Bureau of Education for the Handicapped, U.S. Office of Education, 1969.

Montessori, M. *The Montessori Method.* (A. E. George, Trans.) New York: Frederick Stokes, 1912.

Morgan, S. A. *The Montessori Method: An Exposition and Criticism.* Toronto: L. K. Cameron, 1913.

Norsworthy, N. *The Psychology of Mentally Deficient Children.* Unpublished doctoral dissertation, Columbia University, 1906.

Nowery, J. E. A. "A Brief Synopsis of Mental Deficiency." *American Journal of Mental Deficiency.* January 1945, 352.

Odell, C. W. "Provisions for Mentally Atypical Pupils." *University of Illinois Bulletin,* 1931, *29* (6), 59.

Rogers, A. C. "Functions of a School for Feebleminded." In I. C. Barrows (Ed.), *Proceedings of National Conference of Charities and Correction.* Boston: Ellis, 1888.

Rosewater, A. *Minimum Competency Testing Programs and Handicapped Students: Perspectives on Policy and Practice.* Washington, D.C.: Institute for Educational Leadership, George Washington University, 1979.

Rousseau, J-J. *Rousseau's Emile.* (Wm. H. Payne, Trans.) New York: Appleton, 1896.

Seguin, E. *Theory and Practice of the Education of Idiots.* Paris: L'Hospice de Incurables, 1841.

Seguin, E. *Idiocy and Its Treatment by the Physiological Method.* New York: Teachers College, Columbia University, 1907.

Simches, G., and Bohn, R. "Issues in Curriculum: Research and Responsibility." *Mental Retardation,* 1963, *1,* 84–87.

Steinback, C. "Report of the Special Class Department, Cleveland, Ohio." *Journal of Psychoasthenics,* September 1918, p. 104.

Stevenson, J. A. *The Project Method of Teaching.* New York: Macmillan, 1921.

Wallin, J. E. W. *The Education of Handicapped Children.* Boston: Houghton Mifflin, 1924.

Wallin, J. E. W. *Education of Mentally Handicapped Children.* New York: Harpers, 1955.

Whipple, H. D. *Making Citizens of the Mentally Limited.* Bloomington, Ill.: Public School Publishing Company, 1927.

White House Conference on Child Health and Protection. *Special Education for the Handicapped and Gifted.* Sect. III. *Education and Training.* New York: Century, 1931.

Windle, C. "Prognosis of Mental Subnormals." *American Journal of Mental Deficiency,* March 1962 (monograph supplement).

Witmer, L. *The Special Class for Backward Children.* Philadelphia: Psychological Press, 1911.

Woodrow, H. *Brightness and Dullness in Children.* Philadelphia: Lippincott, 1923.

Herbert Goldstein is a professor of educational psychology in the Department of Educational Psychology, Program in Special Education, New York University.

*Content structures, developmental arrangements, and
cognitive processes are interactive dimensions of curriculum.
The product-process flow model and the participatory group
model represent two exemplary approaches for translating
these dimensions into curriculum materials.*

Two Models for Developing Curriculum Materials

Warren E. Heiss

Curriculum development has as its purpose the organizing of subject matter structures into instructional packages suitable for use with defined groups of learners. Bloom, Hastings, and Madaus (1971) emphasize that the structures of subject matter do not translate directly into structures for learning the subject matter. There is no question that curriculum developers must have a knowledge of the structure of the subject matter, but they must also be able to devise appropriate vehicles for transmitting that structure to learners. This translation of the knowledge of subject matter structures into manageable teaching-learning sequences is the cornerstone of curriculum research and development in special education.

In the preparation of instructional materials, attention must be given to three interlocking dimensions: content—what is to be taught; sequence—the developmental ordering of the content (Kohlberg and Mayer, 1972); and process—how the content is to be presented (Heiss, 1977; Heiss and Mischio, 1971). Recent approaches to curriculum development in special education have concentrated on defining

H. Goldstein (Ed.). *New Directions for Exceptional Children: Curriculum Development for Exceptional Children*, no. 6.
San Francisco: Jossey-Bass, June 1981

appropriate content while attending to the learning characteristics of the target groups and to careful specification of developmental arrangements for presenting content.

Curriculum content defines the information base transmitted through instructional activities as a function of the needs of special groups of learners. Several federally funded projects have defined relevant content for youngsters in special educational settings, among them:

- The Social Learning Curriculum (Goldstein, 1975) offers activities for developing social and affective abilities through the use of inductive teaching procedures.
- Project MATH (Cawley and others, 1975) presents appropriately designed activities for teaching arithmetic to a wide variety of youngsters with learning handicaps.
- I CAN (Field source . . . , 1974) contains instructional units in the areas of physical education, recreation, and leisure skills for use in a variety of special education settings.
- Me Now (Biological Sciences . . . , 1974), Me and My Environment (Biological Sciences . . . , 1974) Me in the Future (1979) consist of instructional activities in the life sciences which have been constructed to emphasize problem solving skills using an inquiry approach.

In addition to defining the content of the curriculum and the ways of organizing and delivering it, each of these projects created an operational system for the production of materials (Mayer, 1975). The purpose of this chapter is to compare and contrast systems or technologies by which curriculum has been developed. Toward this end, the Social Learning Curriculum and the Me Now, Me and My Environment, and Me in the Future projects of the Biological Sciences Curriculum Study (BSCS) will be used as exemplars of contrasting procedures. The development of the Social Learning Curriculum was guided by a model of operation best understood as a product-process flow model. Various curriculum units produced by the Biological Sciences Curriculum Study were managed within a contrasting, participatory group model.

To understand the similarities and differences of these two approaches, a generalized model of curriculum development will be used as a reference point. Both the Social Learning Curriculum and the BSCS projects operated within the general framework illustrated in Figure 1.

Figure 1. Generalized Model for Describing the Curriculum Dimensions of Content, Development, and Process

Content: Social and affective (Social Learning Curriculum)
Biological sciences (BSCS projects)

Development: Sociological (Social Learning Curriculum)
Cognitive (BSCS projects)

Process: Inductive (Social Learning Curriculum)
Inquiry skills (BSCS Projects)

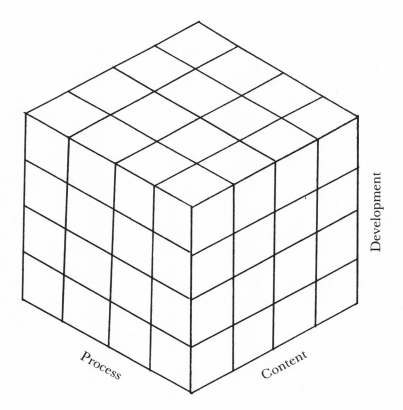

Note: For each curriculum, the number of subdimensions varies, depending on the complexity of each dimension.

The major dimensions of the model shown in Figure 1 are content, development, and process. By defining each of these carefully, the curriculum developer has a structure within which to operate. Once these operational dimensions are specified, the activities of writing the curriculum, evaluating the curriculum, and revising the curriculum can take place.

In the following pages, the product-process flow approach and the participatory group approach to curriculum development will be described. The descriptions will place particular emphasis on how the dimensions of curriculum development are defined and how the writing and revising of curriculum occurs.

Defining Dimensions of the Curriculum

Content Dimension. Irrespective of their commitment to a particular development process, all curriculum development projects must define the scope of the content to be included. In the projects cited, each group of developers approached this task in a different manner.

For the Social Learning Curriculum, the product-process flow began with an attempt to define the nature of the content of the curriculum. Because no existing organized body of knowledge comparable to mathematics or science was available, it became necessary to create a base of information from which to operate. This was accomplished through a needs assessment procedure that undertook to describe problem areas faced by retarded adults (Goldstein, 1967). Data from the needs assessment were organized to define clusters of behaviors that could serve as a basis for defining curriculum content.

The basic task for the developers of the Social Learning Curriculum was to translate the structure defined by the needs assessment into instructional sequences. It was important in this process that the needs assessment and curriculum development activities were conducted by the same in-house group. In essence, the needs assessors became the curriculum developers.

An equally productive approach for delineating the content dimension was taken by the BSCS project staff, who used a participatory group model. Because the BSCS had a successful history in the development of instructional materials for teaching science and because science content is a matter of record, its existing method of operation was adapted for the creation of curriculums for use by special educators. The BSCS curriculum system of development has been fully described by Mayer (1976).

Table 1. Science Content of the BSCS Projects
as Reflected by the Titles of Instructional Units

Me Now	Me and My Environment	Me in the Future
Digestion and Circulation	Exploring the environment	Metrics
Respiration and body wastes	Self as an environment	Agribusiness
Movement, support and sensory perception	Transfer and cycling of materials	Natural resources
Growth and development	Energy relationships	Construction
	Water and air	Manufacturing
		Personal services
		Public services
		Transportation
		Sports
		Nature
		Crafts
		Homes and furnishings
		Self mobility
		Communication
		Personal hygiene
		Raising children
		Food management
		Clothing management

As the first step in defining the content dimension for the BSCS projects, a participating advisory committee was established. The advisory committee included university teachers and researchers in special education, science, and science education. Decisions about the scope and sequence of content of the curriculum emerged from this group's deliberations. Special educators provided information on the relevancy of content for the target group, while science educators and scientists suggested ways of translating this content into meaningful activities that preserved scientific accuracy. In other words, the advisory committee took existing subject matter structures from the biological sciences and distilled pertinent concepts for the curriculum from those structures. The actions of this participating group resulted in the content definition shown in Table 1.

Developmental Dimension. Definition of content results in a collection of themes or topics from which curriculum developers proceed to establish the curriculum's information base. A structure or framework is needed that gives order to the developmental arrangement of such themes.

In the case of the Social Learning Curriculum, the structure of the subject matter was such that the curriculum developers viewed the need area clusters as behavioral realms that maintained their integrity throughout the life cycle. This perspective requires that a developmental sociological framework be used to organize the curriculum. This framework is best seen as a series of expanding environments with which a person must contend.

The developmental levels of self, home and family, neighborhood, and community define contexts in which the curriculum developer will begin to design instructional activities. At this point, a relationship exists between the defined content and the developmental arrangements for that content.

In the product-process flow model, curriculum developers conduct a literature search to locate data relevant to the introduction of concepts at given age levels. Such data provide the curriculum developer with an empirical base for instructional activity design. The use of this developmental model for curriculum development is fully explained by Goldstein (1969).

The BSCS Advisory Committee also had to decide on a developmental arrangement for curriculum content. In this case, however, developmental sequencing was tied to a cognitive flow. In essence, negotiation took place between special educators and scientists. Special educators defined the needs of the target groups with regard to science knowledge, while scientists defined how a given concept could be presented meaningfully. Through this process, advisory committee members were able to structure the instructional activities of the BSCS projects in a developmental order.

Three basic developmental segments were defined. (A fourth segment—Me First—was proposed but not developed.) The three segments were titled Me Now, Me and My Environment, and Me in the Future. While decisions regarding the placement of the BSCS projects in a cognitive developmental order occurred across content areas (that is, content ranged from digestion and circulation to energy and agribusiness), scrutiny reveals that nearly all topics from the three segments are interrelated. This interrelationship provides an expanding conceptual base for the subject matter structure.

Process Dimension. The third dimension of the curriculum teaching-learning process must be defined before actual production of materials can begin. The process dimension entails a paradigm of the learning characteristics of the target group.

An inductive teaching procedure was employed by the developers of the Social Learning Curriculum. This procedure was selected because evidence collected in earlier research showed that inductive techniques were useful in teaching educable mentally retarded youngsters (Goldstein, Mischio, and Minskoff, 1969).

Establishing a particular pedagogical system for the creation of instructional activities allows a curriculum developer to plan a careful sequence of events that offers teacher and learner a programmatic way for reaching concept generalizations. Inductive methodology requires instruction to progress through five stages (Goldstein, 1975). These stages have been described by Heiss (1977, pp. 5–7) in the following manner:

- *Labeling*—questions which elicit the identities of the major components of what is to be explored, such as names of objects or actions
- *Detailing*—questions which elicit the attachment of specific characteristics to major components, such as size, color, position, or quantity
- *Inferring*—questions which elicit a hedged conclusion regarding the function or condition of a major component based on appropriate labeling and detailing; a possibility statement
- *Predicting*—questions which elicit responses about the inference when additional data are made available. These questions often take the form of "What if?" and have as their objective commitment on the part of the student to a conclusion or solution; a probability statement.
- *Generalizing*—following a series of prediction questions, the elicitation of a response of a conceptual nature that provides the child with a category or classification for the major components under consideration.

At this point in the product-process flow model, the inductive methodology variable is entered for the curriculum developer's consideration. All three curriculum dimensions are now defined— social learning content, sociological development, and inductive method.

Historically, the BSCS promoted the use of inquiry skills and problem-solving behaviors as process variables in its materials, so these structures were adopted in the process of creating instructional activities for use in BSCS special education projects. Given the nature of the target group, advisory committee members called for careful delineation of these skills and behaviors so that the curriculum writers could have specific operational definitions to guide them in instructional activity development.

Inquiry skills and problem-solving behaviors are fully described in BSCS documents (Bishop, 1978; Callahan, 1979). Inquiry skills include: observing (accumulating information by using the senses), describing (writing or describing observations orally), identifying (providing a name for the observed phenomenon), comparing (inspecting two or more observations for their differences and similarities), associating (organizing information by developing relationships among observations), inferring (extrapolating beyond the evidence at hand), applying (using what has been learned in a new situation), and predicting (estimating what should happen in a given situation based on prior experience).

Six problem-solving behaviors are embedded in the BSCS projects: identifying the problem, generating possible solutions, formulating a hypothesis, testing the hypothesis and collecting data, reviewing the data and drawing conclusions, and receiving feedback on the success or failure of the conclusion.

For the BSCS curriculum writers, inquiry skill and problem-solving behavior frameworks were defined by BSCS staff members and entered into the formulations for activity development. The three dimensions of curriculum development for the BSCS projects were then in place. The content dimension was represented by biological science, the developmental dimension by a cognitive hierarchy, and the process dimension by inquiry skills and problem-solving behaviors.

Thus, it can be seen that both the product-process flow model and the participatory group model must attend to basic curriculum dimensions. The product-process flow model used to develop the Social Learning Curriculum relied heavily on in-house professionals to determine content, developmental arrangements, and the process characteristics of the curriculum. In general, the product-process flow model places the responsibility for writing the curriculum on the people who develop its basic constructs.

As evidenced by the BSCS participatory group model, curriculum development places responsibility for the development of basic constructs on an active advisory committee. The task of the advisory committee's is to put all the basic groundwork into place. This groundwork is translated by BSCS staff members into formulations to be used by writing teams.

Up to this point, both the product-process flow model and the participatory group model involve the same ingredients for writing curriculum: delineation of content, specification of a developmental arrangement, and definition of a process dimension.

Writing the Curriculum

When the dimensions of curriculum development are clearly defined, the writing of instructional activities can begin. In essence, the writing of instructional activities is the act of making the dimensions of the curriculum framework operational.

In the case of the Social Learning Curriculum, the creators of the instructional activities were, for the most part, also responsible for specifying the dimensions of the curriculum. The interaction of these dimensions lays the foundation for the writer. That is, the writer must, for example, design an intructional activity that addresses the content dimension of *emotional stability* at the developmental level of *self* by employing the *labeling* and *detailing* stages of induction.

Besides attending to these dimensions, the curriculum writer must use a specific format to present the activity. This format includes a statement of objectives; a description of needed instructional materials and teacher preparation; strategies for conducting the activity, including an instructional script; and additional suggestions that expand on the activity.

A curriculum writer working within the framework of the product-process flow model is responsible for producing an entire series of activities arranged as an instructional unit. In this situation, the characteristic flavor of an entire instructional unit is a function of the activity flow that the writer designs.

Development of instructional activities within the framework of the participatory group model involves the use of writing teams. For the BSCS projects, these teams consisted of special educators and science educators. To structure the writing tasks for these teams, BSCS staff members provided formulas based on the curriculum dimensions agreed to by the advisory committee.

The BSCS staff created the skeleton for projected instructional activities. In this situation, a writing team would be asked, for example, to design two activities that attend to *movement of the arm* while developing the inquiry skill of *comparing* and the problem-solving behavior of *collecting data*. All instructional activities were defined by BSCS staff and assigned to writing teams for production. A format similar to that created for the Social Learning Curriculum was used in the BSCS projects.

After the writing teams completed their work, BSCS staff members organized the activities for inclusion in the appropriate instructional units. Refinements and adjustments were made in the instructional activities by BSCS staff members. The participatory group model allowed BSCS staff to act in an advisory capacity to writing teams. Advice was provided in both content and special education matters.

Revising the Curriculum

Once the initial curriculum product is completed, it is subjected to field testing. A major purpose of field testing is to provide evaluation data for use in curriculum revision. Data regarding content, developmental ordering, and process characteristics are collected.

In the case of the product-process flow, field-test evaluation data generated by use of the curriculum are given to each developer. The developer uses these data to alter instructional activities to meet the field-test demands. Adjustments may be made with regard to the content, developmental ordering, or cognitive demand of a given activity.

While much the same process is also used in the participatory group model, some variation is in evidence. Field-test evaluation data are collected and given to both staff members and advisory committee members. The nature of these data can be seen from various BSCS reports (Gromme, 1975). BSCS staff members and the advisory committee members used evaluation data to decide on the revisions required. The dimensions of content, developmental arrangement, and process were all accounted for in this procedure. Once the decisions regarding revision were made, writing teams were constituted to redevelop instructional activities.

Summary

Translating the structure of subject matter into viable instructional products is the task of curriculum development projects. Such translation requires that the dimensions of content, development, and process be clearly established. These three dimensions interact to shape the character of a given curriculum.

Operational models for producing curriculum materials are an outgrowth of the extent to which the dimensions of content, development, and process need to be established. Two models of operation have been described in this chapter. While their objectives were similar , their development processes were different, because their approach to curriculum content, organization, and the processes relevant to content was also different.

As exemplified in the development of the Social Learning Curriculum the product-process flow model resulted from a need to start from scratch in assembling a content base. All curriculum development activity grew from the necessity for generating that base, and a relatively large in-house staff had to be maintained in order to design, write, and revise curriculum materials. This self-contained unit followed the development of the curriculum product through all the processes involved in completion.

In contrast, development of the BSCS projects was governed by a participatory group model. Use of this model for producing curriculum was a function of existing content bases (biological sciences) and an existing process dimension (inquiry skills and problem-solving behaviors). It remained for the BSCS projects to organize participating groups who acted in an advisory capacity and wrote instructional activities. These participants applied existing BSCS configurations to the new problem of creating science curriculums for use in special education settings.

High-quality curriculum materials must convert a subject matter structure into a structure for teaching that is developmentally arranged and that attends to the cognitive skills of the learners. Both the product-process flow model used to produce the Social Learning Curriculum and the participatory group model used by the Biological Sciences Curriculum Study represent efficient, sophisticated systems for meeting these demands of curriculum development.

References

Biological Sciences Curriculum. *Me Now.* Northbrook, Ill.: Hubbard Scientific, 1974.

Biological Sciences Curriculum. *Me and My Environment.* Northbrook, Ill.: Hubbard Scientific, 1977.

Biological Sciences Curriculum. *Me in the Future.* Boulder, Colo.: Biological Sciences Curriculum Study, 1979.

34

Bishop, J. L. *First Formative Evaluation Report: Me in the Future.* Boulder, Colo.: Biological Sciences Curriculum Study, 1978.

Bloom, B. S., Hastings, J. T., and Madaus, G. F. *Handbook on Formative and Summative Evaluation of Student Learning.* New York: McGraw-Hill, 1971.

Callahan, W. P. "Science for the Mentally Retarded: Goals and Assumptions." *The Biological Sciences Curriculum Study Journal*, 1979, *2* (3), 3–5.

Cawley and others. *Project Math: A Program of the Mainstream Series.* Wallingford, Conn.: Educational Sciences, 1975.

Field Service Center for Physical Education and Recreation for the Handicapped. *I Can: Health and Fitness.* Northbrook, Ill.: Hubbard Scientific, 1974.

Goldstein, H. *Cluster Analysis of Problems of Adult Retardates.* New York: Curriculum Research and Development Center in Mental Retardation, Yeshiva University, 1967.

Goldstein, H. "Construction of a Social Learning Curriculum." *Focus on Exceptional Children*, 1969, *1* (2), 1–10.

Goldstein, H. *The Social Learning Curriculum.* Columbus, Ohio: Merrill, 1975.

Goldstein, H., Mischio, G. S., and Minskoff, E. *A Demonstration-Research Project in Curriculum and Methods of Instruction for Elementary Level Mentally Retarded Children.* New York: Yeshiva University, 1969.

Gromme, R. *Assessing Student Abilities and Performance, Year 2: Formative Evaluation Report 4.* Boulder, Colo.: Biological Sciences Curriculum Study, 1975.

Heiss, W. E. "Relating Assessment to Instructional Planning." *Focus on Exceptional Children*, 1977, *9* (1), 1–12.

Heiss, W. E., and Mischio, G. S. "Designing Curriculum for the Educable Mentally Retarded." *Focus on Exceptional Children*, 1971, *3* (2), 1–10.

Kohlberg, L., and Mayer, R. "Development as the Aim of Education." *Harvard Educational Review*, 1972, *42* (4), 449–496.

Mayer, W. V. (Ed.). *Planning Curriculum Development.* Boulder, Colo.: Biological Sciences Curriculum Study, 1975.

Mayer, W. V. "The BSCS Process of Curriculum Development." *BSCS Newsletter*, 1976, *64*, 4–10.

Warren E. Heiss is a professor in the Department of Communication Sciences and Disorders, Montclair State College, Upper Montclair, New Jersey. He was development coordinator for the Social Learning Curriculm and a member of the advisory committee for the Biological Sciences Curriculum Study projects.

Field testing new curriculums is a way to determine whether
innovations are being used appropriately before *attempts*
are made to assess the impact on student performance.

Implementing a Curriculum Field-Test Model

Marjorie T. Goldstein

Caveat emptor! Until recently, that was the message given to consumers by producers of many goods and services. Today, the requirements for products and services are often specified by regulatory
agencies, and compliance is monitored. In education, the field-testing
of products, processes, and ideas has been one response to the need
for greater consumer protection. With the innovations in special
education of the 1960s, field-testing began to assume importance
both for the developers and for the consumers of curriculum products.

What Is Field Testing?

Field testing may be defined as the process by which an
educational innovation developed in one organization (or one part of
an organization) is implemented by a representative group of consumers as one step in validating the innovator.
Educational Innovations. Rogers and Shoemaker (1971) defined
innovation as a product, process, or idea perceived as new by users.

H. Goldstein (Ed.). *New Directions for Exceptional Children: Curriculum Development for Exceptional Children,* no. 6.
San Francisco: Jossey-Bass, June 1981

Several typologies of educational innovations have been proposed (Dalin, 1973; Miller, 1967; Pincus, 1974). These typologies have common themes: organization and administration, human relationships, and instructional content and methods. Curriculum field tests incorporate two concepts of innovation, since they combine a process innovation (field testing), which deals with organization, administration, and human relationships, and a product innovation (curriculum), which deals with instructional content and methods.

Developer Organization/Consumer Organization. The origin of an innovation influences the methods to be used for field testing. The situation in which an innovation is developed in one part of an organization for implementation in another part of the same organization presents different field-test issues from the situation in which the developer organization and the consumer organization are distinct and separate entities. In the latter instance, it is probable that the organizations have different missions, different problems and problem-solving mechanisms, different motives for their actions, and different procedures for attaining their goals.

If we view innovation as one specific type of change (Miles, 1964; Zaltman, Florio, and Sikorski, 1977), it is possible to apply Havelock's (1969) models of change to educational organizations. Havelock evolved three models: social interaction; Research, Development, and Diffusion (RD&D), and problem solving. The social interaction approach is concerned primarily with individuals' influence on change. The RD&D and problem-solver approaches both relate change to group behavior; for this reason, they have greater application to change efforts initiated in educational organizations. According to Havelock, the RD&D approach generates innovations that emanate outside the prospective consumers' organizations, with limited participation by consumers prior to diffusion of the innovation. The problem-solver approach focuses almost exclusively on processes that occur within the consumer organization: identifying and ordering problems, searching out and evaluating alternative solutions, and selecting the most promising alternative for trial implementation. Havelock contends that a synthesis of the three models is needed, since developer and consumer organizations and the individuals who comprise them all have the potential to influence the change process.

In the past decade, several special education curriculum innovations have been developed through R&D centers (H. Goldstein, 1974), colleges and universities (Bieberly, Lent, and Keilitz, 1974;

Field Service Unit for Physical Education and Recreation for the Handicapped, 1974; Cawley and others, 1975), and private organizations (Biological Sciences Curriculum Study, 1974). The field testing of these curriculums required developer and consumer organizations to collaborate. Levine and White identified this concept as *organizational exchange*, which they defined as "any voluntary activity between two organizations which has consequences, actual or anticipated, for the realization of their respective goals or objectives" (1960, p. 586).

Facilitating Validation. A growing body of research on the implementation of educational innovations indicates that developers' assumptions that their creations are being used appropriately by consumers are often unwarranted (Goodlad and others, 1970; Gross, Giacquinta, and Bernstein, 1971; Stallings, 1974). Several analyses of implementation efforts (Berman and McLaughlin, 1975; Carlson, 1965; Gross, Giacquinta, and Bernstein, 1971) suggest that cases in which unsupervised implementation results in failed innovation are, in fact, cases of faulty implementation. To overcome this problem, field testing lays a foundation of appropriate implementation as a precursor to evaluation. Field testing is not an evaluation process; instead, it links an innovation with a representative group of users and supports their implementation efforts, thus making evaluation possible.

Assumptions About Field-Testing

Three assumptions underlie an organizational exchange field-test model. The first assumption is that educational organizations differ from other types of formal organizations (Bidwell, 1965) and that certain differences, such as tenure, unionism, and compulsory attendance laws, can affect the ways in which such organizations respond to innovation (Owens and Steinhoff, 1976).

The second assumption is that organizations, not individuals, are the initial unit of decision making when an innovation is introduced into an educational system. This is especially true in special education, where teachers are spread among the schools in a system and where program leadership is located at some distance from the teachers. This situation contrasts with that of general education, where the unit of organizational change most often cited is the individual school (Fullan, 1972; Havelock, 1973; Gross, Giacquinta, and Bernstein, 1971) and where the innovation advocate deemed pivotal to the innovation attempt is the school principal (Gross, Giacquinta, and Bernstein, 1971; Sarason, 1971). We may note here that the principal is frequently responsible for the special education classes located in his or her school, and the result is that special education teachers often serve two masters—the principal and the special education leader. Studies have shown that teachers cannot introduce significant innovations into the system without support from local leaders, since implementation of most innovations requires resources that are beyond the control of the individual teacher (Berman and McLaughlin, 1975; Fullan, 1972; Gross, Giacquinta, and Bernstein, 1971; Kievit, 1975). Taken together, these factors suggest that the introduction of innovations into special education programs may represent distinctly different problems than those created by innovation in general education; indeed, innovations in special education may be more difficult to achieve.

The third assumption is that the needs and goals of the developer organization are different from the needs and goals of the schools that consume its products. The needs of the developers are governed to a large degree by the innovation being created. In contrast, the schools have a continuing mandate to educate the pupils in their charge. This mandate cannot be set aside while decisions are made to introduce an innovation. An innovation that is not viewed by the system as facilitating the achievement of its mandate is often eschewed, since the innovation is not seen as contributing to current functioning. Thus, it is important to examine the needs of both organizations to identify, and subsequently to achieve, some commonly valued goal. Examination occurs most directly at the outset of field-testing, but it continues to some extent throughout the period during which the developer and consumers are engaged in organizational exchange.

An Organizational Exchange Model for Field-Testing

To simplify the discussion that follows, the term *developer* is used to refer to the organization from which the innovation emanates. *Consumers* are the school districts or other educational organizations where the innovation is introduced and field tested. Members of the developer group include the curriculum developers, evaluators, researchers, and field-test staff. The consumer group includes local administrators, supervisors, and implementors of the innovation.

An organization exchange field-test model (Figure 1) was developed to accommodate the different needs and goals of developer

Figure 1. Organizational Exchange Field-Test Model

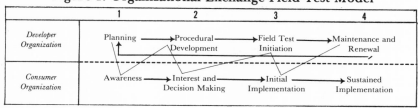

and consumer organizations as they engage in field testing. The developer organization field-test model is based on work by M. T. Goldstein (1976). The actions ascribed to the consumer organization are drawn from Zaltman, Duncan, and Holbek's (1973) model of the innovation process in organizations and from an elaboration of the process by Zaltman, Florio, and Sikorski (1977) specific to education.

Figure 1 illustrates a four-phase process for developers and consumers. The developer phases are planning, procedural development, field-test initiation, and maintenance and renewal; the consumer phases are awareness, interest and decision making, initial implementation, and sustained implementation. The coupling of a developer phase with a consumer phase, such as planning with awareness, represents a stage. While each organization can lay the foundations for field testing independently by following the phases in sequence, ideally the actions of developers and consumers are reciprocal in that action by one group influences action or response by the other. The discussion that follows describes each stage to provide an integrated view of the field-test process.

Planning. At the outset, to determine whether there is a need to field-test their innovation, the developers examine two related factors: the routineness or radicalness of the innovation and the attributes of the innovation. If the developers decide to proceed with field testing, these same two factors influence the form and substance of the field test. Planning for a field test involves establishing a unit within the developer organization to coordinate field testing, identifying the population of prospective consumers and determining relevant demographic variables, and examining practical factors affecting site selection.

Routine/Radical Innovations. According to Knight (1967), innovations can be classified as *routine* or *radical*. Routine innovations are built into the functioning of the organization. For example, the reevaluation and replacement of textbooks by substituting a more current text after a specified number of years is a routine innovation. In contrast, radical innovations require changes in role relationships or significantly alter teachers' instructional behavior. Examples of radical educational innovations include the introduction of a new curriculum covering a subject not previously taught, individualized instructional programs, or open education.

Innovation Attributes. Users' perceptions of the attributes of innovations have received much attention in the literature on diffusion and implementation (Hahn, 1973; Rogers and Shoemaker, 1971; Wyner, 1974; Zaltman, Duncan, and Holbek, 1973; Zaltman, Florio, and Sikorski, 1977). Rogers and Shoemaker (1971) identified five attributes that they conceived to be applicable to all types of innovation: relative advantage, compatibility, complexity, trialability, and observability. Relative advantage, the degree to which the innovation is perceived to be an improvement over what it replaces, is an important attribute at the point when consumers become aware of the innovation. Compatibility, the degree to which the innovation is perceived to be congruent with existing values, past experience, and the needs of the consumer, is important when consumers engage in decision making about the innovation. Complexity is the degree to which the innovation is perceived to be difficult to understand and to use. Trialability is the degree to which the innovation is perceived to be implementable on a limited basis. Observability is the degree to which the results of the innovation are perceived to be visible to others. The last three attributes are of concern to consumers when they begin to implement the innovation.

The developer's decision concerning the need to field-test is based on their view of whether the innovation requires radical behavior change by implementors and by the program into which the innovation is introduced. This view, in turn, depends on the developers' perception of the specific attributes of the innovation.

Field Coordination. A field-test unit that is part of the developer organization serves as a bridge between developers and the consumers who participate in the field test (M. T. Goldstein, 1976). The staffing of this unit depends on the scope and structure of the field test to be conducted. The field-test unit provides the major communication linkage between developers and consumers, assuring consistency of communication and increasing the speed and accuracy with which messages are communicated to and from consumers. This unit also assumes responsibility for training field-test participants and for monitoring appropriate use of the innovation by implementors.

Demographics, Sampling, and Size. Joint decisions are made by members of the developer group concerning the types of data to be collected and who is to provide the data. Initially, the targeted consumer population for the innovation must be identified, and the demographic characteristics of the sample necessary to ensure generalizability of results must be specified. Based on the array of demographics, the size of the field-test sample can be determined. At this time, the initial training needs of implementors are also considered; particular attention should be given to identifying the prerequisite skills needed to implement and evaluate the innovation (M. T. Goldstein, 1976).

Practical Factors. Once the target population has been identified, practical factors that facilitate or constrain field testing in naturalistic settings can be examined. Among the factors that should be considered are: the location of the special education program within the district's organizational structure, with attention to the extent of autonomy in decision making and control of budget; the roles and role relationships among professionals within the program; and the district's history of innovation attempts (Zaltman, Florio, and Sikorski, 1977). Experience supports the view that information about these factors, in combination, is useful to predict a school district's general capability to engage in field testing.

More specific program information can include the size of the special education program, the type of leadership available to the special education program and how it is deployed, and the alternative placement options available to provide education and related services to students.

Awareness. While the developers are still engaged in planning activities, they devise strategies to create awareness that the innovation exists among prospective consumers. Newsletters, journal articles, and presentations at professional meetings are typical dissemination tactics (Mayer, 1975; Rogers and Svenning, 1969). While these tactics have been found to have limited impact on producing changed behavior among listeners (Rogers and Svenning, 1969; Turnbull, Thorn, and Hutchins, 1974), they are valuable as a means of creating awareness about innovations. Such tactics can serve to provoke potential consumers to seek additional information about an innovation. Particularly important during the awareness phase is the consumers' perception of the relative advantage of the innovation over current practice. The developer's role is to create interest in the innovation and to lay a foundation for further exploration with the consumer organization.

Procedural Development. Work done during the planning stage leads logically to the formulation of practices and procedures to facilitate field-testing. The major activities are structuring the field test and preparing guidelines to govern consumers' participation. The developers' objectives are to structure field testing so that it is functional and cost-effective and to specify what is expected of consumer organizations.

Structuring the Field Test. Centralized or decentralized organizational patterns may be selected when structuring a field test. If the innovation represents an alteration of content in a field that is well grounded in research and theory and that has a history of prior curriculum development, such as math or science, there may be less need for sampling diversity, and the scope of the field test can be reduced. In such cases, a centralized field test would offer a parsimonious field-test structure. However, if the innovation to be field tested incorporates sociocultural phenomena, such as social skills or career education, and if it lacks a structure based on extensive theory, research, and curriculum development, a decentralized field-test structure is more appropriate. A decentralized structure allows developers to accommodate anticipated differences in implementor and student reactions to the materials due to social and cultural differences (H. Goldstein, 1978). Such a structure allows for participation by several school districts, each reflecting differernt sociocultural perspectives on the innovation. Thus, the selection of an appropriate structure is based on the substance of the innovation and on the demographics that determine the scope of the field test.

Centralization places day-to-day management of the field test with the developer's field-test unit. Decentralization locates day-to-day management of field testing within the consumer organization, with a corresponding loss of control over certain implementation variables by the developer. Selection of a field-test structure determines the professional staff within the consumer organization that will participate in field testing. A centralized field test requires that the developers emphasize selection of implementors of the innovation. A decentralized field test requires that the developers emphasize selection of a local field-test manager as a preliminary step to the joint selection of field-test teachers. The field-test manager assumes general responsibility for the conduct of the field test at the site. It is best if the regular workload of the person selected as field-test manager overlaps considerably with the activities that are part of the field-test manager's role (M. T. Goldstein, 1976). In large measure, the field-test manager determines the degree of success that school district and teachers experience with field testing, since this individual acts as the primary local advocate for the innovation.

Finally, communication channels are needed to ensure the systematic flow of information to and from consumers. Developers assume responsibility for managing communication flow for centralized field tests. A more elaborate communication system is needed for decentralized field tests, since more people are involved. Likert's (1961) link pin model, which relies on specified role incumbents in an organization to provide inter- and intragroup communication, is an appropriate means for establishing communication channels in decentralized field tests. Likert's model relies on overlapping group communication systems at all levels of the organization where communication moves from its source to those who need the substance of the communication in order to function effectively in a planned and orderly way (Schmuck and others, 1972).

Figure 2 shows how developer-consumer communication channels can be organized to facilitate a decentralized field test. The developer's field-test coordinator and the consumer's field-test manager and teachers are the primary participants. The figure also shows the secondary channels that have potential to serve as sources of information and support: college and university personnel and regional and state personnel. These sources are not tied directly to the

Figure 2. Field-Test Communication Channels

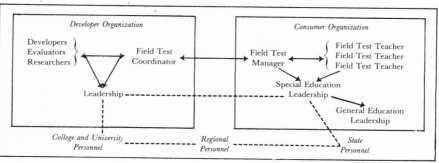

developer organization or to the consumer organization. Nonetheless, where some aspect of field testing overlaps an area of their interest or concern, these sources can facilitate field testing. Intermediate between the primary and secondary field-test communicators are the leaders of both organizations, who provide administrative support and material resources for the conduct of the field test.

Developing Operational Guidelines. Codifying procedures into a set of guidelines (M. T. Goldstein, 1974) to facilitate consumers' partici-pation in field-testing is the final step of this phase. Guidelines are the most useful if they specify criteria for site selection; procedures for field test initiation, maintenance, and renewal; and procedures to be used in collecting research and evaluation data. Guidelines that include as much operational detail as possible allow developers to make their expectations of consumers' performance explicit and prospective consumers to make informed decisions about involving their organization in field testing.

Interest and Decision Making. Interest in curriculum innovations is typically generated in schools through the use of print materials, personal interaction, inservice training, or a combination of these approaches (Mayer, 1975; Rogers and Svenning, 1969). To bridge the gap between interest and decision making, it is important for someone within the district to act as internal advocate for the innovation. If this individual occupies a leadership position, he or she is better able to generate interest in the innovation among prospective implementors (Berman and McLaughlin, 1975; Gross, Giacquinta, and Bernstein, 1971; Hall, 1974; Havelock, 1973; House, 1974; Wayland, 1964). Once prospective implementors express interest in the innovation, the advocate seeks formal approval for the conduct of the field test, in all its particulars, from the organization's leadership. (The procedural guidelines for field-testing are especially useful to the advocate in stating the case for involvement in field testing.) Concurrently, group and individual decision making occurs among prospective imple-mentors and their supervisors. Research confirms that individuals who participate in decisions concerning their work tend to be more motivated, more productive, and more satisfied with the work in which they engage (Argyris and Schon, 1974; Herzberg, 1966; Zaltman, Florio, and Sikorski, 1977). Experience indicates that before implementors commit themselves to field testing, they consider the innovation's attributes, the personal and professional consequences of field-test involvement, and the extent to which the innovation will have a positive impact on their students' progress.

The interest and decision-making phase culminates at the point when a go-no go decision is reached by the school district's administration and communicated to the developer organization. Closely linked to this action is the designation of a field-test manager and the tentative identification of implementors. Commitments can be formalized by contractual agreement (Mayer, 1975), or they can be informally agreed upon by parties representing both organizations (M. T. Goldstein, 1976). At this point, the groundwork has been laid for field-testing.

Field Test Initiation

Site Selection. Procedural guidelines form a useful basis for selecting field-test sites. Sites are drawn from the population for which the innovation is developed. Sites should include a sufficiently representative sample to allow generalizability of the results of the field test (M. T. Goldstein, 1976; Mayer, 1975). Often, school districts that seek involvement in an innovative activity like field-testing display certain characteristics: openness to innovation, a history of innovation attempts, recognition of the relative advantage of the innovation for their schools, and flexibility of internal procedures that allows them to meet criteria set for field-test participation (Greenwood, Mann, and McLaughlin, 1975; Widmer, 1977).

Training. The importance of training those engaged in innovative educational efforts is well documented (Berman and McLaughlin, 1975; Gross, Giacquinta, and Bernstein, 1971; Lippett and others, 1967; Sarason, 1971; Turnbull, Thorn, and Hutchins, 1974; Zaltman, Florio, and Sikorski, 1977). Training for field-test participants begins when they receive orientation to the innovation and continues, through use of systematic training and feedback procedures, for the duration of the field test (M. T. Goldstein, 1976).

Joyce and Showers (1980) identified two purposes for staff development in the schools: to fine-tune skills already possessed and to expand the repertoire of instructional behaviors by mastering new skills. When a field test is being conducted, a related purpose for staff development is mastering of skills associated with evaluation of the innovation (M. T. Goldstein, 1976). Joyce and Showers (1980) contend that mastery of new skills requires more intensive training than fine-tuning since the magnitude of desired behavior change is greater. Therefore, curriculum innovations that require mastery of a range of knowledge and skills for appropriate implementation and evaluation can require training that extends over a period of time so that users have opportunities for distributed practice in using and evaluating the innovation (Mayer, 1975). If training is provided at regular intervals, incremental gains in teachers' proficiency in implementing and evaluating field-test materials are possible, since the same broad training time frame can provide mastery and fine tuning of both types of skills.

Most often, the recipients of field-test training are implementors of the innovation and the internal advocate who supports their implementation efforts (M. T. Goldstein, 1974; Mayer, 1975). Training for implementors is directed toward their attaining mastery in using and evaluating the innovation (M. T. Goldstein, 1976). Training for internal advocates has been effective in helping them to create conditions in which the innovation can be initiated and maintained (Fullan, 1972; Gross, Giacquinta, and Bernstein, 1971) and in increasing their capability to deal with systemic problems associated with introduction of the innovation (M. T. Goldstein, 1974; Havelock, 1973; Wayland, 1964). Training for internal advocates has also been found to have long-range benefits for the installation of innovations. Mahan (1972) and Turnbull, Thorn, and Hutchins (1974) found that after the novelty of implementation wears off, the continued interest and assistance provided by the organization's leaders becomes an important motivator for continued use of the innovation by teachers.

An important element in assessing the impact of field-test training is the extent to which observed user behaviors are consistent with developer specifications of appropriate teaching behaviors associated with the innovation (Fullan and Pomfret, 1977). Both curriculum-specific measures (Evans and Scheffler, 1974; Warshow and Bepko, 1974; Warshow, Smith, and Goldstein, 1976) and generic approaches (Hall, Wallace, and Dossett, 1973; Hall and Loucks, 1977) have been used to obtain this information. These approaches to assessment of teachers' use of an innovation are useful as indicators of teachers' readiness to evaluate it. Training teachers in evaluation skills often follows the same pattern as training for implementation. While it is possible to incorporate both implementation and evaluation skills into initial training programs (M. T. Goldstein, 1976), experience has shown that separate training yields a more positive result, since participants can concetrate on developing implementation and evaluation skills in turn and refining their skills in each area over time.

Initial Implementation

Consumer System. The field-testing of curriculum innovations incorporates implementation as a prior step to curriculum evaluation. This stands in contrast to many innovations that reportedly never reach the implementation stage (Fullan and Pomfret, 1977; Goodlad and others, 1970; Sarason, 1971). The initial implementation period represents the consumers' first efforts to operationalize the field test on site. Mahan (1972) found that "thorough planning and thorough execution of curriculum installations are rare events" (1972, p. 146). To overcome this problem, it is possible to initiate field-testing on a small scale in order to fit the innovation to the site. Small-scale field testing can involve limiting the number of participants, the duration of the commitment to field-testing, and the expenditure of human and material resources allocated to field-testing (M. T. Goldstein, 1974; Zaltman, Florio, and Sikorski, 1977). This enables consumers to concentrate their resources on fewer participants and to limit the disruption caused by the introduction of an innovation into their system (Zaltman, Florio, and Sikorski, 1977). A conservative approach allows consumers to assess the viability of the curriculum innovation and of field testing in their organization without undue disruption of the system as a whole.

The complexity of initiating innovation in the schools is well documented (Berman and McLaughlin, 1974; Fullan and Pomfret, 1977; Gross, Giacquinta, and Bernstein, 1971; Goodlad and others, 1970, 1974; Sarason, 1971). The literature emphasizes preparation, timing, organizational climate, available resources, and participants' attitudes and motivation. Other complexities arise from requirements that are peculiar to field-testing during the initial implementation phase. Thus, as Mayer (1975) notes, developers need to consider extending field-test time frames so that sites have time in which to make any necessary adaptations to the field-test process and effect a good fit with the ongoing procedures of the organization.

Field Test Manager. As local advocate for the innovation, the field-test manager is responsible for overseeing the progress of the field test. A predictable period of disequilibrium occurs when an innovation is introduced into a system (Hall, 1974). This disequilibrium is in proportion to the magnitude of the change effort (Miller, 1969). It is likely, therefore, that the innovation advocate bears the brunt of the disruption of the system. For this reason, the innovation advocate requires the support of others similarly committed to the innovation if problems associated with initial implementation are to be overcome (Greenwood, Mann, and McLaughlin, 1975; Wayland, 1964). Thus, there is a need for strong internal advocacy for the innovation at different levels in the educational hierarchy, particularly at the outset (Greenwood, Mann, and McLaughlin, 1975; Gross, Giacquinta, and Bernstein, 1971; Havelock, 1973; House, 1974; Sarason, 1971).

The types of strategies and tactics used by advocates to introduce curriculum innovations into educational systems have been studied (Berman and McLaughlin, 1974; M. T. Goldstein, 1979; Turnbull, Thorn, and Hutchins, 1974). Three broad kinds of change strategy have been identified: the rational, the persuasive, and the coercive (Chin and Benne, 1969; Hull and Kester, 1975; Sieber, 1972). A recent study by M. T. Goldstein (1979) reported that of these three strategies, persuasive strategies that included advocates' use of normative-reeducative tactics were positively related to teachers' implementation of a curriculum innovation. Support was found for advocates' use of demonstration tactics in which opportunities were provided for teachers to observe the innovation in use and to become involved in adapting the innovation to local conditions.

Implementors. While local leaders may influence intitial decision making about field-test involvement, individual teachers are the ultimate implementors of curriculum innovations. Hall, Wallace, and Dossett (1973) devised a Concerns-Based Adoption Model to classify the concerns expressed by teachers when confronted with a new situation that requires them to modify some aspect of their teaching performance. Three types of concerns were identified: self concerns—the individual's personal concerns about the task that he or she is expected to perform; task concerns—the mechanics of mastering the professional tasks required; and impact concerns—the individual's projected assessment of the impact of the innovation on student performance.

Similar concerns have been expressed by teachers when they prepare to field-test. Strategies to allay teachers' concerns may be incorporated in the orientation of teachers to field-testing. However, it is only after teachers begin to use the curriculum and gain confidence in using it with students that concerns begin to abate. The initial implementation phase provides a period when teachers can experiment with the innovation. Berman and McLaughlin (1974) describe this as a mutual adaptation process: Teachers shape the innovation to their educational setting and to their particular teaching style. M. T. Goldstein (1979) reported that advocacy tactics associated with mutual adaptation were related positively to the degree of implementation by teachers of a curriculum inovation. However, others (Carlson, 1965; Fullan, 1972; Goodlad and others, 1974) caution that adaptation of the innovation requires careful monitoring lest teachers' implementation becomes so distorted that the innovation is unrecognizable to its developers.

Two important sources of feedback for field-test teachers are students and the field-test manager. Experience indicates that positive student reaction to the innovation tends to reinforce and sustain teachers' initial implementation efforts. Feedback from the field-test manager is often more structured and specific to the innovation. In sum, the initial implementation phase serves as a period of adjustment for the school district, the field-test manager, and the field-test teacher, and it lays the foundation for sustained implementation and evaluation of the curriculum innovation.

Maintenance and Renewal. Maintenance and renewal of field-test efforts are viewed as simultaneous, not sequential, actions (M. T. Goldstein, 1976). Maintenance actions facilitate day-to-day field-test coordination; renewal actions modify field-test operations in response to changed needs and new situations (M. T. Goldstein, 1976). Gardner (1961, 1963) described maintenance and renewal and noted that both types of action are critical to an organization's ability to adapt and change in order to continue to function productively in its environment. By including maintenance and renewal as elements of the same phase, the developers can establish stable procedures for field-testing while at the same time creating a cycle of planning and adaptation activities to improve productivity.

Maintenance. Maintenance actions provide stability and predictability for field-test participants. There are three broad categories of field-test maintenance actions: materials support, consultative and training support, and communication support.

Materials support addresses the flow of field-test materials to and from participating sites. Alternative systems for dissemination of materials exist. The system selected will depend on the developer's needs and finances. The mechanics of materials management are important to the field-test process. As simple an accommodation as stamped self-addressed envelopes can contribute substantially to the rate of return of curriculum evaluations and other materials from field-test sites. The timing of the distribution of materials also is important for developers, since the planning and execution of this activity adds predictability to field-testing by meeting consumers' expectations for receipt of field-test materials in a timely fashion.

Consultation and training that follows the initiation of field-testing provides participants with the technical assistance needed to implement and evaluate the innovation. Two types of training are provided by developers: One type is initiated by the developers when they identify some aspect of field-test performance that needs to be strengthened, and the other is provided in response to consumers' needs. Training initiated by the developers is most often directed to mastery and fine-tuning of skills associated with implementation or evaluation of the innovation. In addition to training for teachers, it is useful to offer staff development for field-test managers. Staff development for field-test managers should provide opportunities to engage in leadership training specific to the innovation as well as training that is more general and applicable to their roles in their school districts (M. T. Goldstein, 1976). Training requested by consumers can be broadly focused on integrating the innovation into other aspects of the local program and the particular setting in which it is used. The goal of consultation and training provided by developers, beyond competent implementation and evaluation of the innovation, is for the school district to adopt the proven innovation as part of its ongoing program.

Communication is, in actuality, the overriding linkage function and incorporates both materials support and consultation and training. The two-way communication established between the developer and consumer organizations permits information to flow quickly from those who have it to those who need it in order to function. Regular communication with field-test sites that is responsive to their particular needs is basic to the success of the organizational exchange.

Renewal. Renewal provides the mechanism for continuously evaluating, planning, and implementing modifications in the field-test process. When a field test is planned to extend over several years, it is possible that some procedures will become outmoded or even dysfunctional after a period of time (M. T. Goldstein, 1976). Thus, regular examination of routine procedures is needed. Renewal offers opportunities for all field test participants to contribute vitality to the field-test process. It allows curriculum developers, evaluators, and researchers to create new and better ways of gathering information and of having the changes implemented smoothly. As Goldstein notes, "Continuity of field-test sites and of the field-test process is based on establishing a balance between maintenance and renewal functions. The goal is to manage a field test that is adaptable to both internal and external change" (M. T. Goldstein, 1976, p. 32).

Sustained Implementation. If the initial implementation phase has been successful for consumers, it is likely that they will continue to implement the innovation (Zaltman, Duncan, and Holbek, 1973). Since field-testing incorporates implementation as a prior step to curriculum evaluation, sustained implementation of the innovation for the duration of the field test is all but assured. Attention may, therefore, be directed to measuring the extent and quality of implementation.

The selection of particular measures of implementation depends on the content of the curriculum innovation and on the developers' evaluation objectives. Curriculum developed for content areas that are well grounded in theory and prior curriculum development can focus on the fidelity of users' implementation, an approach identified by Fullan and Pomfret (1977). Here, evaluators will want to see whether teachers implement the curriculum as written. In contrast, where curriculum is developed for areas that lack prior developmental structuring of content, evaluators will be concerned with validating the appropriateness and relevance of content. Such evaluations will approximate the process approach (Fullan and Pomfret, 1977).

As the mechanics of field testing become routine, participants can devote more time to fine tuning their skills. As field-test managers gain confidence with the innovation and with the administrative procedures associated with field testing, their roles become more substantive. They become sensitive to the quality of teachers' participation and to teachers' attitudes toward field testing. They work to assist teachers to fine-tune teaching skills needed to implement the innovation effectively. In this way, field-test managers become internal change agents (Havelock, 1973; Zaltman, Florio, and Sikorski, 1977) and local resources for information and assistance concerning the innovation.

As the capacity of the site to develop its local expertise increases, control of the field test shifts from the developer to the consumer organization (M. T. Goldstein, 1976). This shift creates local independence without the loss of developer support. Too, increased independence of field-test sites from the developer improves the validity of curriculum evaluation by allowing field-testing to be as naturalistic as possible (M. T. Goldstein, 1976). As local sites increase their sense of ownership of the innovation through greater local control of the field test, participants are encouraged to identify ways for improving the field-test process. The organizational exchange is enhanced by reciprocal feedback systems that allow renewal efforts to be initiated by all who are involved in the process. Since one major objective of the developers is to obtain information that can serve as a basis for evaluation, the open communication established through field-testing increases the probability that this goal will be realized.

Summary

The organizational exchange field-test model described in this chapter elaborates a process through which the developer's need to field-test and evaluate an innovation and a consumer's need to keep current with changes in the field can be merged. This model is also applicable to the introduction of curriculum innovations in a school district where field-testing is not the prime objective, as in the case of commercially prepared materials or in a situation where the innovation was developed in the district where it is to be implemented. While the amount of emphasis given to each stage in the process varies both with the innovation and with the school district's objectives, the principles that support the use of a thoughtful planning-to-implementation strategy are the same.

References

Argyris, C., and Schön, D. A. *Theory in Practice: Increasing Professional Effectiveness.* San Francisco: Jossey-Bass, 1974.

Berman, P., and McLaughlin, M. W. *Federal Programs Supporting Educational Change.* Vol. I: *A Model of Educational Change.* Santa Monica, Calif.: Rand, 1974.

Berman, P., and McLaughlin, M. W. *Federal Programs Supporting Educational Change.* Vol. IV: *The Findings in Review.* Santa Monica, Calif.: Rand, 1975.

Bidwell, C. E. "The School as a Formal Organization." In J. G. Marsh (Ed.), *Handbook of Organizations.* Chicago: Rand McNally, 1965.

Bieberly, C. J., Lent, J. R., and Keilitz, I. *How to Do MORE.* Bellevue, Wash. Edmark Associates, 1974.

Biological Sciences Curriculum Study. *Me Now.* Northbrook, Ill.: Hubbard Scientific, 1974.

Carlson, R. O. *Adoption of Educational Innovations.* Eugene, Ore.: Center for the Advanced Study of Educational Administration, 1965.

Cawley, J. F., and others. *Project Math: A Program of the Mainstream Series.* Wallingford, Conn.: Educational Sciences, 1975.

Chin, R., and Benne, K. D. "General Strategies for Effecting Changes in Human Systems." In W. G. Bennis, K. D. Benne, and R. Chin (Eds.), *The Planning of Change.* (2nd ed.) New York: Holt, Rinehart and Winston, 1969.

Dalin, P. *Strategies for Innovation in Education.* Vol. IV: *Case Studies of Educational Innovation.* Paris: Center for Educational Research and Innovation, Organization for Economic Cooperation and Development, 1973.

Evans, W., and Scheffler, J. "Degree of Implementation: A First Approximation." Paper presented at annual meeting of the American Education Research Association, Chicago, April 1974.

Field Service Unit for Physical Education and Recreation for the Handicapped. *I Can: Health and Fitness.* Northbrook, Ill.: Hubbard Scientific, 1974.

Fullan, M. "Overview of the Innovative Process and the User." *Interchange,* 1972, *2* (3), 1–46.

Fullan, M., and Pomfret, A. "Research on Curriculum and Instruciton Implementation." *Review of Educational Research,* 1977, *4* (2), 335–397.

Gardner, J. W. *Excellence.* New York: Harper and Row, 1961.

Gardner, J. W. *Self-Renewal: The Individual and the Innovative Society.* New York: Harper and Row, 1963.

Goldstein, H. *The Social Learning Curriculum, Level I.* Columbus, Ohio: Merrill, 1974.

Goldstein, H. "Publishing and Marketing a Curriculum for Special Education." In *Excerpts: The National Marketing Conference on Special Education.* Westerville, Ohio: LINC, 1978.

Goldstein, M. T. *Field-Test Advisor Guidelines (Revised).* New York: Curriculum Research and Development Center in Mental Retardation, Yeshiva University, 1974.

Goldstein, M. T. *Field-Testing: A Model and Its Applications.* New York: Curriculum Research and Development Center in Mental Retardation, Yeshiva University, 1976. (ERIC Document No. ED 157 223)

Goldstein, M. T. "Diffusion Tactics Influencing Implementation of a Curriculum Innovation." Unpublished doctoral dissertation, Yeshiva University, 1979.

Goodlad, J. I., and others. *Behind the Classroom Door.* Worthington, Ohio: Charles A. Jones, 1970.

Goodlad, J. I., and others. *Looking Behind the Classroom Door.* Worthington, Ohio: Charles A. Jones, 1974.

Greenwood, P. W., Mann, D., and McLaughlin, M. W. *Federal Programs Supporting Educational Change.* Vol. III: *The Process of Change.* Santa Monica, Calif.: Rand, 1975.

Gross, N., Giacquinta, J. B., and Bernstein, M. *Implementing Organizational Innovations: A Sociological Analysis of Planned Educational Change.* New York: Basic Books, 1971.

Hahn, C. L. "Relationships Between Potential Adopters' Perceptions of New Social Studies Materials and Their Adoption of Those Materials in Indiana and Ohio." Unpublished doctoral dissertation, Indiana University, 1973.

Hall, G. E. *The Concerns-Based Adoption Model: A Developmental Conceptualization of the Adoption Process Within Educational Institutions.* Austin: Research and Development Center for Teacher Education, University of Texas, 1974.

Hall, G. E., and Loucks, S. F. "A Developmental Model for Determining Whether the Treatment Is Actually Implemented." *American Educational Research Journal,* 1977, *14* (3), 263–276.

Hall, G. E., Wallace, R. C., and Dossett, W. D. *A Developmental Conceptualization of the Adoption Process Within Educational Institutions.* Austin: Research and Development Center for Teacher Education, University of Texas, 1973.

Havelock, R. G. *Planning for Innovation Through Dissemination and Utilization of Knowledge: Final Report.* Ann Arbor: Center for Research on Utilization of Scientific Knowledge, Institute for Social Research, University of Michigan, 1969.

Havelock, R. G. *The Change Agent's Guide to Innovation in Education.* Englewood Cliffs, N.J.: Educational Technology Publications, 1973.

Herzberg, R. *Work and the Nature of Man.* New York: World, 1966.

House, E. R. *The Politics of Educational Innovation.* Berkeley, Calif.: McCutchan, 1974.

Hull, W. L., and Kester, R. J. *Perceived Effectiveness of Innovation Diffusion Tactics.* Columbus: Center for Vocational and Technical Education, Ohio State University, 1975.

Joyce, B., and Showers, B. "Improving In-service Training: The Messages of Research." *Educational Leadership,* 1980, *37* (5), 379–385.

Kievit, M. B. "Technology for Children: A Case Study of a Development and Diffusion Effort." Paper presented at annual meeting of the American Education Research Association, Washington, D.C., 1975.

Knight, K. "A Descriptive Model of the Intrafirm Innovation Process." *Journal of Business,* 1967, *40,* 478–496.

Levine, S., and White, P. E. "Exchange as a Conceptual Framework for the Study of Interorganizational Relationships." *Administrative Science Quarterly,* 1960, *5,* 583–601.

Likert, R. *New Patterns of Management.* New York: McGraw-Hill, 1961.

Lippett, R., and others. "The Teacher as Innovator, Seeker, and Sharer of New Practices." In R. I. Miller (Ed.), *Perspectives on Educational Change.* New York: Appleton-Century-Crofts, 1967.

Mahan, J. M. "Frank Observations on Innovation in Elementary Schools." *Interchange,* 1972, *3* (2–3), 144–160.

Mayer, W. V. (Ed.). *Planning Curriculum Development: With Examples from Projects for the Mentally Retarded.* Boulder, Colo.: Biological Sciences Curriculum Study, 1975.

Miles, M. B. (Ed.). *Innovation in Education.* New York: Teachers College, Columbia University, 1964.

Miller, R. I. "Some Observations and Suggestions." In R. I. Miller (Ed.), *Perspectives on Educational Change.* New York: Appleton-Century-Crofts, 1967.

Miller, R. I. "The Role of Educational Leadership in Implementing Educational Change." *California Journal for Instructional Improvement,* December 1969, pp. 221–232.

Owens, R. G., and Steinhoff, C. R. *Administering Change in Schools.* Englewood Cliffs, N.J.: Prentice-Hall, 1976.

Pincus, J. "Incentives for Innovation in the Public Schools." *Review of Educational Research,* 1974, *44* (1), 113–144.

Rogers, E. M., and Shoemaker, F. F. *Communication of Innovations: A Cross-Cultural Approach.* New York: Free Press, 1971.

Rogers, E. M., and Svenning, L. *Managing Change.* San Mateo, Calif.: Operation PEP, 1969.

Sarason, S. B. *The Culture of the School and the Problem of Change.* Boston: Allyn and Bacon, 1971.

Schmuck, R. A., and others. *Handbook of Organization Development in Schools.* Palo Alto, Calif.: National Press Books, 1972.

Sieber, S. D. "Images of the Practitioner and Strategies of Educational Change." *Sociology of Education,* 1972, *45,* 362–385.

Stallings, J. "An Implementation Study of Seven Follow Through Models for Education." Paper presented at annual meeting of the American Education Research Association, Chicago, 1974.

Turnbull, B. J., Thorn, L. I., and Hutchins, C. L. *Promoting Change in Schools: A Diffusion Casebook.* San Francisco: Far West Laboratory for Educational Research and Development, 1974.

Warshow, J. P., and Bepko, R. A. *The Social Learning Environment Rating Scale.* New York: Curriculum Research and Development Center in Mental Retardation, Yeshiva University, 1974.

Warshow, J. P., Smith, I. L., and Goldstein, M. T. *SLOR Manual: A Guide to Using the Social Learning Observation Record.* New York: Curriculum Research and Development Center n Mental Retardation, Yeshiva University, 1976.

Wayland, S. R. "Structural Features of American Education as Basic Factors in Innovation." in M. B. Miles (Ed.), *Innovation in Education.* New York: Teachers College, Columbia University, 1964.

Widmer, J. L. "Innovation and Bureaucracies: A Reexamination of Diffusion Strategies for State and Local Systems." Paper presented at annual meeting of the American Education Research Association, New York, 1977.

Wyner, N. "A Study of Diffusion of Innovation: Measuring Perceived Attributes of an Innovation That Determine the Rate of Adoption." Unpublished doctoral dissertation, Columbia University, 1974.

Zaltman, G., Duncan, R., and Holbek, J. *Innovations and Organizations.* New York: Wiley, 1973.

Zaltman, G., Florio, D., and Sikorski, L. *Dynamic Educational Change: Models, Strategies, Tactics, and Management.* New York: Free Press, 1977.

Marjorie T. Goldstein is special education consultant at Educational Improvement Center/Northeast in West Orange, New Jersey. From 1969 to 1978, she was coordinator of field operations at the Curriculum Research and Development Center in Mental Retardation at Yeshiva University and New York University where she gleaned much of the information on which this chapter is based.

*With public demand for accountability in education and the
end of massive infusions of federal funds into educational
research and development, evaluation assumes critical
importance for the curriculum developer.*

The Role of Evaluation
in the Development of Curriculum

Raymond A. Bepko

The purpose of this chapter is to present a model for a practical
working relationship between curriculum developers and evaluators.
The goal is to enable readers to adapt and apply this model to their
own setting. By the end of the chapter, readers should understand the
model well enough to decide whether further consideration is
warranted.

Some Basic Concerns

Long neglected or, at best, relegated to second rank by educational program developers, the field of curriclum evaluation came
into its own in the 1960s. With the publication in 1967 of Scriven's
perspectives of curriculum evaluation and the American Educational
Research Association monograph series (1967) that it inaugurated,
theoretical and methodological developments occurred with great
rapidity. While many significant events in curriculum evaluation
occurred prior to the mid sixties, the last fifteen years have seen a

H. Goldstein (Ed.). *New Directions for Exceptional Children: Curriculum Development for Exceptional Children*, no. 6.
San Francisco: Jossey-Bass, June 1981

profusion of methodologies, techniques, and technologies. This evaluation explosion has sometimes been characterized by heated debate over the purposes, nature, and proper role of evaluation in the context of curriculum development.

Evaluation and Research. An unobtrusive measure of the place of evaluation in the development of curricula is to be found in the very names of the agencies at the forefront of educational innovation. Most are called research and development (R&D) centers. Most often, evaluation has been seen as secondary to development and as an adjunct to or responsibility of the research team (Sax, 1974; Stake, 1975). The evaluation function has not been accorded as vital a place as its development and research counterparts. In addition to its possible contribution to the sense of insecurity among evaluators, it can be argued that the semantic designation does not reflect the operational reality. While research activities play a major role in laying the foundation for curriculum, evaluation activities are equally critical in the framing and finishing of the product.

Research and evaluation in curriculum development are similar in that they engage in the collection, analysis, synthesis, and interpretation of data. They may utilize identical or similar designs, approaches, and methods for each of these four activities. Research and evaluation differ not in the ways in which information is gathered but in their use of information. From this perspective (Borich, 1974), the primary purpose of research is to provide information for the validation of a theoretical position. The primary purpose of evaluation is to provide information for making decisions about product or process.

Evaluation Concepts. Scriven (1967, 1977) asserts that the basic goal of evaluation is to answer a limited number of questions about a given entity: How well does it perform? Is it better than the alternatives? Is it worth it? Answering these questions is the goal, regardless of the entity under consideration. Hypothetically, as long as this is kept in perspective, it hardly matters what role evaluation assumes, whether as part of a teacher-training program, a curriculum development project, or an ad hoc committee that selects schools to be closed. The same primary concerns must be addressed.

Sax (1974, p. 3) defines evaluation as "a process through which a value judgment or decision is made from a variety of observations and from the background of the evaluator." Sax's definition highlights two central characteristics of evaluation: the formulation of value judgments and the importance of the evaluator's background (and, by implication, biases) in the formulation of that judgment. This contrasts with Scriven's argument that the evaluation process is abstract and independent of the subject being evaluated.

Quay (1977) takes the issue further when he asserts that evaluators ought to be as concerned with product as with process, as focused on the what as on the how. While he certainly does not deny the importance of procedural and design questions, Quay believes that evaluation must take factors related to a program's integrity into account before a judgment about its merit is rendered. These factors include the clarity of the program's conceptual base; the services actually delivered; the level of expertise, training, and supervision of delivery staff; and the characteristics of the population being served.

To some extent, then, program integrity is a prerequisite for program evaluation. Rutman (1977) makes just this point when he suggests that three preconditions must be met in planning an evaluation: a clearly articularted program, clearly specified goals or effects, and a rationale that links the program to the goals or effects.

Stake (1975) identifies another area of concern: the necessity for evaluators to be responsive to the audience of the evaluation. He emphasizes learning about the needs of this audience so that they may be noted when reporting program effects. He criticizes many evaluation plans for too strongly stressing goal and objective statements, objective tests, and research-type reports. He believes that responsive evaluation is oriented more to program activity than to program intent. Stake observes that evaluations are expected to accomplish many different objectives, each of which necessitates the collection and analysis of different sets of data. Rather than attempting to meet overblown expectations, he implies, evaluation ought to emphasize only a few prime questions determined by assessment of the needs of the evaluator's audience. Hence, we arrive once again at Scriven's primary concerns.

The concept of curriculum evaluation that is advanced in this chapter and upon which the model to be presented is predicated is as follows. Beyond the issues of experimental design, statistical procedure, and reliable measurement lies the primary purpose of curriculum evaluation: improvement of the curriculum while it is being developed. From this perspective, the goals and the roles of evaluation are inextricably linked. Two other questions are prerequisite to Scriven's three: What ought to be known about the material? Why is that knowledge important? The answers to these questions can result in rational evaluation plans, strategies, and procedures. The questions themselves require evaluation to be closely involved with development of the curriculum from the very inception. This fact has obvious implications for the types of evaluation to be conducted within the context of a curriculum production effort. In sum, evaluation will be viewed in this chapter as systematic and continuous assessment of an educational product and process, the curriculum, for the purposes of its revision and modification and of decision making. This is primarily a formative conceptualization of evaluation, which leads us to the next issue.

Types of Evaluation. The divisions reflected in the debates concerning the relation of evaluation and research are repeated in the controversy over the kind of evaluation to be conducted in an educational setting. In his seminal work on the evaluation of educational programs and products, Borich (1974) argues that formative and summative conceptualizations reflect different ways in which techniques are used rather than differences in techniques themselves. The parallel to the research-evaluation discussion is obvious. Formative evaluation is concerned with obtaining information for developers to use in program or product revision. Summative evaluation is concerned with providing information to consumers that will help them to make a decision about adopting the program or product. According to Borich, the formative and summative positions are most clearly "expressed as states of mind, viewpoints, or perspectives rather than techniques or points in time" (1974, p. 273). Formative evaluation can occur when the possibility exists of improving the program or product. Most often, it produces data on the various components of this program or product (Rutman, 1977). Summative evaluation usually occurs after revisions have been made and no further substantial improvement is likely (Cronbach, 1977). It produces data on the effects of the whole program; often, it compares these effects with the effects of alternative products. Thus, the bottom line for formative evaluation is the production of information that assists in program improvement (Baker, 1974). For summative evaluation, the bottom line is the production of information that enables accurate decision making regarding the finished product.

Distinctions between formative and summative evaluation other than temporal ones have a way of vanishing. Scriven (1967) argues that curriculum evaluation must and inevitably does make use

the group of people for whom the curriculum is intended. The *somewhere* is the physical, social, and psychological environment in which the teaching-learning transactions occur. The *somehow* is the instructional methodology tied to the content of each program or curriculum component.

Evaluation activities have traditionally focused on two of these elements, the target population and the content of instruction. Less often, consideration is given to the instructional methodology, and even less often to the program implementor and environmental background. It is rare when the interrelationships among all five elements are considered in an evaluation effort.

The importance of considering all five elements has been emphasized by several investigators. Glennon (1973) noted that the failure of a curriculum to produce significant results can be associated with deficiencies in implementation as well as with defects in the program itself. The implication is that comparative data on student outcomes are relatively limited in their utility without data on curriculum implementation. Rosenshine and Furst (1973) emphasized the relationships among teacher behavior, implementation strategies, and pupil gains. Further, a consideration of all five elements in the teaching-learning paradigm would appear to be an essential prerequisite for determining the program's integrity (Quay, 1977). Deciding whether there is actually an entity to evaluate—that is, whether the curriculum has been implemented in accord with the intent of its developers—must precede the actual evaluation.

The degree to which the curriculum is implemented in accord with the specifications of the developers can clearly influence the effects of that curriculum on learners. According to Seidel (1978), in its focus on the product, much evaluation fails to see the interpersonal transactions among the curriculum implementors and the population exposed to the curriculum, the features of the environment in which all work, and the effects of environmental, implementor, and population characteristics on actual implementation of the innovative product.

Context. Sax (1974) defines an evaluation strategy as a plan for developing the procedures used to arrive at decisions about students or programs. Such strategies are not developed in a vacuum. Thus, the PDP can only be understood and assessed within the context in which it evolved. The chapters in this volume by Heiss and M. Goldstein present the development and field-test context for the PDP.

A model is useful to the extent that it is precise (avoiding ambiguity), specific in its concerns (avoiding overextension of its premises and promises), and verifiable (avoiding nonempiricism). Borich (1974, pp. 143–153) uses these criteria to review five major evaluation models. The PDP most closely resembles Bertram and Childers' (1974) multistage model for evaluating educational products. Both models are concerned with specification and refinement of objectives, assembly of appropriate methodological packages, data collection, analysis, and interpretation. Both also place the evaluation process within the context of a complete development process. Hence, evaluation is seen as separate but not removed from development. The multistage model, however, emphasizes summative evaluation activities as part of the proper role of project evaluators, while the PDP keeps these roles distinct. Futher, the PDP proposes a more intensive role for evaluators in actual development activities than the Bertram and Childers model.

Perhaps the most salient feature of the PDP is the activist role assumed by evaluators in the development process, from initial planning through final revision. Although some evaluative tasks may in isolation appear to be summative in character, the thrust of evaluation is clearly formative. The model assumes that summative evaluation is important and that it should be conducted—but not be evaluators connected with the development process. The potential for conflict of interest is too great. This position frees the evaluator from unnecessary concern over "cooption" (Baker, 1974) and enables the evaluator to get about the business of producing the best product possible under the circumstances by providing data useful in revising and adapting the product.

Morris and Fitz-Gibbons (1978) describe a general evaluation model that identifies parameters that the PDP shares with other specific models. The four major goals of this general model are: setting the program evaluation boundaries—what the evaluation will and will not attempt to do; preparing a program statement that identifies the aims and methods of the program; monitoring actual implementation of the program and the attainment of program objectives; and reporting results and conferring with program planners and staff.

The PDP provides for each of these goals. Six primary steps for meeting these goals have been described by Fink and Kosecoff (1978): formulating credible questions, constructing evaluation designs, planning information collection, collecting evaluation information, planning and conducting information analysis activities, and reporting evaluation information.

The PDP is successful to the extent that it facilitates completion of these steps and enables evaluators to meet these goals.

The Four Phases of the Model

The Product Development Process model consists of four phases, each comprised of steps that are usually completed in sequence. Figure 1 depicts the PDP flow.

Phase 1: Planning. The interaction between development and evaluation functions begins here. At the completion of this phase, the parameters of the curriculum and the curriculum evaluation should be clear.

Step 1: Define Program Scope. Consistent with established design principles, the developers define the scope and nature of the proposed curriculum product. Evaluators and researchers conduct studies, where necessary, to provide information for developers. The main responsibility for this step lies with the developers, and a working paper is the usual end product.

Step 2: Review the Literature. This review, conducted by all appropriate staff, results in the compilation of information necessary for material design and development activities.

Step 3: Specify Program Parameters. Based upon the literature review, consultation with appropriate experts, and the results of any research or evaluation studies, developers specify the goals and objectives of the proposed curriculum product.

Figure 1. The Product Development Process

Phase I: Planning
1. Define program scope
2. Review literature
3. Specify parameters
4. Identify evaluation needs
5. Specify target population
6. Select and recruit sites

Phase II: Production
7. Draft materials and media
8. Specify information for revision
9. Specify desired outcomes
10. Design evaluation strategy and procedures
11. Decide final evaluation plan

Phase III: Field-Testing
12. Orient program implementors
13. Complete data management plan
14. Activate field-test network

Phase IV. Revision
15. Analyze and interpret data
16. Prepare summary reports
17. Revise program

Step 4: Identify Evaluation Requirements. Development, evaluation, and media personnel meet to review the goals and objectives and to give preliminary answers to the questions "What needs to be known, and why?" and "What data are necessary in order to know it?" This step often results in refinement of goals and objectives into more measurable statements.

Step 5: Specify the Target Population. Developers and evaluators specify the characteristics of the desired target population for field-testing the program—the someone, somebody, and somewhere of the 5S paradigm. Characteristics of subjects, environment, and implementors are specific. Criteria for participation in the field test are set.

Step 6: Select and Recruit Field-Test Sites. The field operations and evaluation personnel use the criteria developed in step 5 to identify possible sites for field-testing. Field-test personnel recruit and select sites for the actual field test and establish a liaison with them by providing preliminary information. For a comprehensive discussion of field operations, the reader is referred to the chapter by M. Goldstein in this volume.

Phase 2: Production. By the completion of this phase, marked by activity specific to the separate functions but characterized also by frequent interaction, everything needed for the field test has been done.

Step 7: Draft Materials and Media. Developers and media personnel complete production of the field-test version of the curriculum component.

Step 8: Specify Information Needed for Revision. Evaluation personnel meet with development and media people to more fully answer the questions initially considered in Step 4. The categories of information necessary for revision of the program materials and media are comprehensively defined.

Step 9: Specify Desired Outcomes. Evaluators, in conjunction with curriculum developers, specify changes desired in the target population as a function of exposure to the curriculum. Outcomes to be assessed during the actual field test are selected. Not all possible outcomes are selected.

Step 10: Design Evaluation Strategy and Procedures. Evaluators specify strategy and outline procedures for field-testing of the program. Studies to be conducted in conjunction with the field test are designed. Evaluators design, develop, select, and pilot instrumentation for gathering data on the target population, the curriculum implementors, the environment in which the curriculum is implemented, and the ways in which the curriculum is implemented.

Step 11: Discuss and Decide on Final Evaluation Plan. Evaluators, in conjunction with the project's development, media, and field test personnel, review studies to be conducted, evaluative data to be gathered, and data-gathering techniques in order to determine whether all information necessary for program revision has been considered and whether the plan is likely to result in obtaining the desired information.

Phase 3: Field Testing. By the end of this phase, all information required for completion of the evaluation has been gathered. The primary characteristic of this phase is close cooperation between evaluation and field-test personnel to monitor and, if necessary, revise the evaluation plan.

Step 12: Orient Program Implementors. Evaluators, field-test personnel, and program developers design an orientation program to be given on site or self-instructional packages to be included with the material itself.

Step 13: Complete Data Management Plan. With field-test personnel, evaluators specify the procedures for receiving data from field-test sites and preparing them for analysis.

Step 14: Activate Field-Test Network. Field-testing of the curriculum material begins. Data are collected. Field observations are conducted. Early in this step, a preliminary review of the data from field-test sites is conducted in order to determine whether field evaluations are of acceptable quality and to identify and resolve any problems incurred in gathering the information.

Phase 4: Revision. In the last phase, evaluators work closely with developers to prepare information that will result directly in program revision.

Step 15: Analyze and Interpret Data. Evaluators discuss with developers issues that emerge from the preliminary data review conducted in step 14 in order to determine relevance for revision. Appropriate statistical analyses are then conducted of evaluation data and data collected in studies in conjuntion with field-testing. Data are interpreted in light of the questions raised in steps 8 and 9.

Step 16: Prepare Summary Reports. Technical reports are prepared and distributed as appropriate. Results are discussed with development and media personnel. Final recommendations for revision are made. Implications for future development efforts are discussed.

Step 17: Revise Program. Project developers make revisions in the curriculum product as indicated by the summary reports and discussions. The revised version is then made available for summative evaluation or for publication.

Summary

Product Development Process presented in this chapter incorporates an evaluation model into a description of the relationships between evaluation and development, media, research, and field operations. The model details each step in the planning, production, field-testing, and revision of a curriculum product. The model has been described in the context of issues surrounding the emergence of curriculum evaluation as a major educational endeavor.

Any application of this model can be evaluated by the degree to which it meets some basic criteria. First, and most importantly, to what extent is the information generated by the model incorporated into revision of the curriculum? Second, does the application of the model result in greater efficiency on the part of curriculum developers in producing the curriculum? Third, does the final version of the curriculum contain a method of evaluation for the curriculum user; that is, does the final package include a means by which consumers of the curriculum can evaluate and modify it to suit their own needs and purposes?

References

American Educational Research Association. *Perspectives of Curriculum Evaluation: AERA Monograph Series on Curriculum Evaluation.* Chicago: Rand McNally, 1967.

Alter, M., and Bepko, R. A. "A Proposal for Curriculum-based Individualized Educational Planning." New York: Curriculum Research and Development Center in Mental Retardation, New York University, 1978.

Baker, E. L. "The Role of the Evaluator in Instructional Development." In G. D. Borich (Ed.), *Evaluating Educational Programs and Products.* Englewood Cliffs, N.J.: Educational Technology Publications, 1974.

Bertram, C. L., and Childers, R. D. "A Multistage Model for Evaluating Educational Products." In G. D. Borich (Ed.), *Evaluating Educational Programs and Products.* Englewood Cliffs, N.J.: Educational Technology Publications, 1974.

Borich, G. D. (Ed.). *Evaluating Educational Programs and Products.* Englewood Cliffs, N.J.: Educational Technology Publications, 1974.

Cronbach, L. "Course Improvement Through Evaluation." In A. Bellack and H. Kliebard (Eds.), *Curriculum and Evaluation.* Berkeley, Calif.: McCutchan, 1977.

Fink. A., and Kosecoff, J. *An Evaluation Primer.* Washington, D.C.: Capitol Publications, 1978.

Glennon, T. K. "The National Institute of Education: A Personal View." Presentation to annual meeting of the American Educational Research Association, New Orleans, February 1973.

Goldstein, H. "Construction of a Social Learning Curriculum." *Focus On Exceptional Children,* 1969, *1* (2), 1–10.

Goldstein, H. "Social Learning: A Curriculum Element in the Education of Retarded Children." Paper presented at meeting of the Ontario Association of Education Administrative Officials, Toronto, February 1974.

Morris, L., and Fitz-Gibbons, C. *Evaluator's Handbook: Program Evaluation Kit 1.* Beverly Hills, Calif.: Sage, 1978.

Quay, H. "The Three Faces of Evaluation: What Can Be Expected to Work?" *Criminal Justice and Behavior,* 1977, *4,* 341–354.

Rosenshine, B., and Furst, N. "The Use of Direct Observation to Study Teaching." In R. Travers (Ed.), *Second Handbook of Research on Teaching.* Chicago: Rand McNally, 1973.

Rutman, L. "Planning An Evaluation Study." In L. Rutman (Ed.), *Evaluation Research Methods.* Beverly Hills, Calif.: Sage, 1977.

Sax, G. *Principles of Educational Measurement and Evaluation.* Belmont, Calif.: Wadsworth, 1974.

Scriven, M. "The Methodology for Evaluation." *Perspectives of Curriculum Evaluation.* American Educational Research Association Monograph Series on Curriculum Evaluation, No. 1. Chicago: Rand McNally, 1967.

Scriven, M. "The Methodology of Evaluation." In A. Bellack and H. Kliebard (Eds.), *Curriculum and Evaluation.* Berkeley, Calif.: McCutchan, 1977.

Seidel, R. *Transactional Evaluation: Assessing Human Interactions During Program Development.* Alexandria, Va.: Human Resources Research Organization, 1978.

Stake, R. "Particularly Responsive Program Evaluation." Occasional Paper No. 5. Kalamazoo: College of Education, Western Michigan University, 1975.

Warshow, J. P., Bepko, R. A., and Becker, J. H. "The Relationship Between Evaluation and Development in a Curriculum Research and Development Center." New York: Curriculum Research and Development Center in Mental Retardation, Yeshiva University, 1975.

Raymond A. Bepko is a psychologist with the Marcy (New York) Psychiatric Center. From 1972 to 1978, he served on the staff of the Curriculum Research and Development Center in Mental Retardation.

A number of functional approaches, principles, procedures,
and tools can be used to manage curriculum development
projects effectively. They will not replace an effective
manager, but they can aid a potentially effective manager.

Managing Curriculum Development

James F. Budde

Every day, as curriculum is being developed, wheels are reinvented, haphazard approaches are taken, energy is expended ineffectively, and those responsible experience stress and frustration. The fact is that, while many of us have been trained to be educators and curriculum developers, few of us have been trained to be managers. Typically, management models used for curriculum development resemble those used for the classroom. Frequently, effective management philosophies are nonexistent. Existing management tools are often relatively crude. Even for those with management prerequisites, management can sometimes be frustrating. However, with a sound management foundation, problems can be made manageable, and curriculum development can become a rewarding and productive endeavor.

Managers of curriculum development systems often view management of curriculum development as a true challenge. In their view, the curriculum development system resembles the assembly line on which sophisticated airplanes are designed, developed, and tested.

H. Goldstein (Ed.). *New Directions for Exceptional Children: Curriculum Development for Exceptional Children*, no. 6.
San Francisco: Jossey-Bass, June 1981

Products of the system are viewed as precision tools that have been designed appropriately, developed systematically, tested thoroughly, and packaged attractively.

Curriculum development systems must be tailored to the type of products that will be developed and the resources that are available. A wise manager will always develop a curriculum development system that is the most practical for the particular situation. Sophistication is rarely the answer.

For this reason, it is appropriate to ask what a practical curriculum development system is. Before attempting to answer this question, it seems appropriate to ask what a curriculum development system is.

A curriculum development system is a production structure that resembles a manufacturer's assembly line. Typically, it contains six components: marketing, needs study, or both; product design; product development; product testing; product packaging; and product dissemination.

What is a practical and functional curriculum development system? Only those responsible for a particular system can answer this question. If the curriculum to be developed is similar to a quarter yard of patching cement, a simple but functional approach is required, but if the curriculum to be developed is similar to two hundred yards of cement that must be delivered daily, a more complex yet practical approach is called for.

The manager or person responsible for the curriculum development system is a key figure in its success. This individual must take a particular set of resources and develop products of a particular quality and quantity. Typically, the circumstances and resources with which this must be done are never ideal. The manager must rely on his skills and judgment in order for the system and its products to be successful.

In order for the curriculum development system to be successful, a sound management process must be applied to the particular situation. If the management process is sound and there are no insurmountable problems, a practical development system can be developed.

How does the manager go about developing a functional curriculum development system? There is a basic sequence of organizational steps that can be applied to all curriculum development:

- defining needs
- establishing goals
- specifying objectives
- developing evaluation questions
- designing curriculum products
- developing curriculum products
- testing and revising curriculum products
- disseminating curriculum products.

First, not all steps will be needed in every system. Most often, however, some approximation of most steps will be required (Mayer, 1975).

Second, each step involves a series of substeps. Each substep can also involve its own series of substeps. Therefore, the manager will need to possess adequate task-analysis and planning skills in order to define and illustrate the numerous steps and their relationships.

Third, every step and substep will be affected by at least five variables: the resources that are available, the level of sophistication, the time that is available, the receptiveness of the surrounding environment, and the motivation of the manager and those with whom the manager works.

Fourth, the manager must be able to anticipate, determine, and deal with these variables. Dealing with these variables is a continuous management process, which includes a sequential and revolving set of management steps that must be applied to each curriculum development step (Budde, 1979). These management steps include:

- Defining the curriculum development problems and steps as tasks;
- Organizing personnel and resources to accomplish these tasks;
- Defining each task and its relationships with other tasks in detail;
- Defining constraints that may impede and resources that may facilitate accomplishment of tasks;
- Developing strategies and resources to accomplish the tasks;
- Developing criteria to select the best options for accomplishing tasks and making the final selection;
- Developing a plan relating subtasks based on the options that were selected for accomplishing tasks;

- Implementing this plan;
- Testing the tasks and subtasks to ensure that they are efficient and effective;
- Using test information to revise and improve the tasks and subtasks.

Fifth, one of the manager's greatest assets is the manager's staff or those who will develop the curriculum. These individuals make or break curriculum development systems. A manager who does not have a good staff has little probability for success.

It may be noted here that not all persons are well suited to be managers. If an individual does not have certain leadership characteristics and is not reinforced by management or motivated to manage, the probability that this individual will be a successful manager is low. Professional training could help, but such efforts typically pay few dividends either for the system or for the would-be manager.

Thus far, this chapter has defined a general rationale for the management of curriculum development, outlined steps for organizing a curriculum development system, and defined steps for managing a curriculum development system. The remainder of this chapter will develop a detailed method for establishing a curriculum development system and describe specific tools and procedures that can be used to manage such a system.

Establishing a Curriculum Development System

What is referred to here as the curriculum development system is more than a development system. It is sometimes called a *curriculum implementation system*, and it has three major components: curriculum design, curriculum development, and curriculum dissemination.

It should be remembered that the curriculum develpment system is a production system. The size and scope of this system depends upon the particular job. Its actual content will depend upon the individuals involved and the unique constraints of their setting.

Models are useful in developing plans for curriculum development systems. For simple systems, an outline is adequate. For complex systems, more precise planning tools are required. Several of these planning tools have been described in detail (Budde, 1979; Silverman, 1972).

The actual planning process involves taking the major components and breaking them down into increasingly smaller components. This is repeated until the desired level of detail is reached.

The General Curriculum Development System. Since no one curriculum development system will suit all purposes, a general plan including several levels of detail will be presented here. Figure 1 illustrates this general plan. The plan contains a number of subcomponents that should be considered when planning a curriculum development system. By no means does it include all possible components.

Planners of a curriculum development system typically start at the top with major goals and work toward the bottom with objectives and tasks. As information is generated through analysis and planning of objectives and tasks, it is then synthesized into the overall plan or system.

The general curriculum development system has three major objectives: curriculum design, curriculum development, and curriculum dissemination.

Curriculum Design. Curriculum design is often viewed as the simplest component. However, the opposite is true. That is, curriculum design is probably the most complex and involved goal and the one about which least is known. It is also probably the most important, because mistakes made at this level have a tendency to plague work throughout the other components.

The curriculum design objective contains three subobjectives: establishing the curriculum field, designing individual products, and conducting feasibility studies.

Establishing the curriculum field involves defining all the curriculum products that could or should be developed. This task involves two subtasks: market identification and development of a curriculum target. Market identification has two components: determining needs—identifying areas where education and training is required—and determining variables—acquiring all relevant information that will affect curriculum development. Development of a curriculum target has three components: analyzing market information to establish a goal, integrating information about needs into content areas, and specifying content areas in which a product can be developed.

The design of individual products involves two tasks: defining product specifications and developing a testing system. Defining

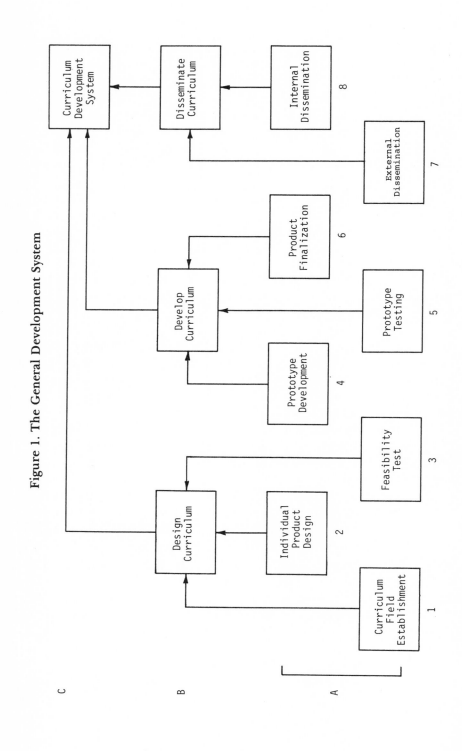

Figure 1. The General Development System

Figure 2. Curriculum Design

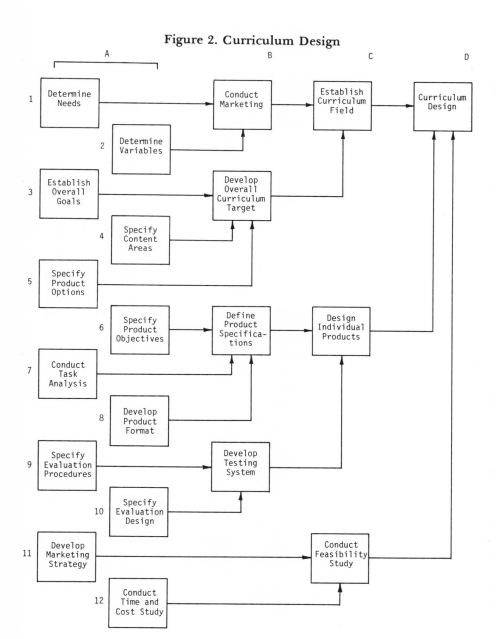

product specifications involves three subtasks: specifying objectives (precise statements about the outcome in terms of knowledge, skills, or behavior), conducting a task analysis (breaking objectives down into steps), and developing a product format (the way in which the content will be presented and packaged). Developing a testing system involves two subtasks: specifying the evaluation design (including evaluation questions, data points, research method, measurement techniques, and test population) and specifying evaluation procedures (including timetable, data collection procedures, and arrangements for testing).

The third subobjective of curriculum design is conducting a feasibility study. The purpose of a feasibility study is to determine whether it is indeed feasible to continue product development. Several decisions can be made after this final design subobjective is reached: to proceed with product development, to terminate product development, to redesign the product, or to acquire additional information. For this reason, the tasks involved in conducting a feasibility study include developing a marketing strategy, which in turn involves determining the best approach for final production and dissemination of the product, and conducting a time-cost study, which acquires information needed to make a final decision about whether the curriculum product can be developed with existing personnel, resources, and time.

Curriculum Development. The curriculum development objective is the step in which the final product is produced. Curriculum development has three subobjectives: prototype development, prototype testing, and prototype finalization. Prototype development is the process of creating the first draft or prototype. Prototype testing is the process whereby the effectiveness and efficiency of this first draft is tested. Prototype finalization results in the finished product.

Developing a product prototype has three subtasks. First, refining the product design calls for refining the task analysis. At this point, the task analysis is redefined to reflect final design modifications, and the final evaluation design is completed. The second task, developing the product content, is an involved step and requires a fair amount of resources and manpower. This step is the actual curriculum development. At this stage, product designs are sometimes scrapped and the task analysis is reanalyzed. The third task, mediating the product prototype, is achieved as the product is being completed.

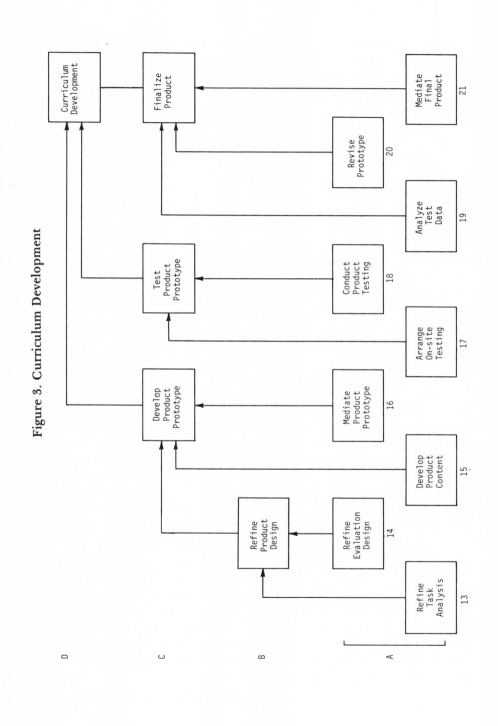

Figure 3. Curriculum Development

Ideally, media support is a continuous system involved in all three objectives: design, development, and dissemination.

Testing the product prototype involves two major subtasks: arranging on-site testing and conducting the product testing. At this point, the product is actually tested, either with on-site subjects or in the field. After test data are collected, it may become apparent that extensive revision, involving further development and testing, is required.

In the final stage of curriculum development, prototype finalization, the final touches are put on the product before dissemination. Finalization is accomplished by analyzing the test data to ensure that the product is ready, revision of the prototype to develop the final product, and mediating the product by on-site media facilities, an independent contractor, or a commercial publisher.

Curriculum Dissemination. The third objective of the general curriculum development system, curriculum dissemination, has two subobjectives: dissemination through an external source and dissemination through an internal source. While some systems use just one of these methods, most use both.

The external souce is usually a publisher, and dissemination through an external publisher includes querying publishers to determine interest in the product, selecting a publisher (this may well include "selling" the publisher), and coordinating publication. Coordinating publication can involve a good bit of work, but this process can begin during the curriculum design objective. Conflicts are to be anticipated if the final product is modified significantly by the publisher.

Dissemination through internal sources typically includes scheduling publication of products and disseminating the final products with the help of such identified or existing resources as mailing lists, curriculum catalogues, and identified users.

It should be noted that the curriculum development system just described does not take time lines or product recycling into account. It merely illustrates goals, objectives, subobjectives, tasks, subtasks, and their relationships. Actually, many of the tasks in a curriculum development system can and do take place simultaneously. Also, there may be one or more products in the system on which tasks are performed simultaneously. Products can be scheduled and rescheduled for various tasks.

Scheduling and monitoring of products, progress, and tasks

Figure 4. The Curriculum Dissemination

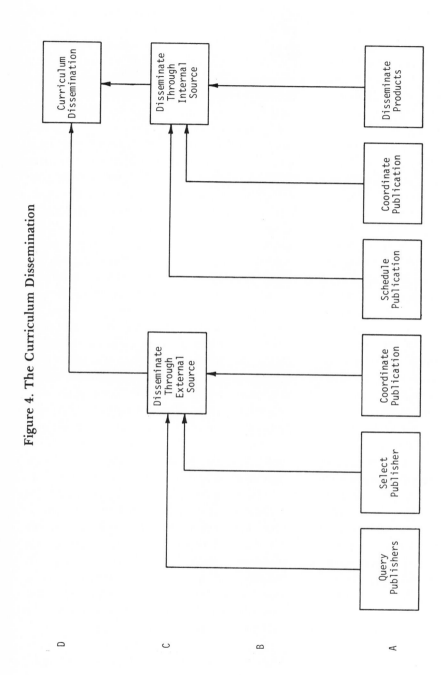

performed are key management functions. How they can be accomplished is described in the next section.

The Management System

The mangement system is an integral part of the curriculum development system. The role that management plays is similar to that of the leader or quarterback of the team. Management should be viewed not as an entity of authority that prevails over the curriculum development system but as a working body that facilitates the curriculum development system. Its function is to lead and sometimes to push the system so that is accomplishes the objectives set out for it. If the curriculum development system is to be an ongoing system, management will need to see that there are products to produce and objectives to achieve in the future.

The preceding section described what could be contained in the curriculum development system. Pre- and postdevelopment management tasks are associated with the establishment of such a system.

Predevelopment management tasks require the formation of a key group of planners to study the environment around and within a proposed curriculum development system. Once the planning process is initiated, tasks involve setting deadlines and keeping the planning process on track. Often, management plans with time lines are developed and used to plan the curriculum development system. (See Figure 5 for an example.) During the planning process, the basic sequence of organizational steps defined earlier should be used to plan the goals, objectives, tasks, and subtasks of the curriculum development system.

Once the plan is completed and resources to develop the curriculum development systems are acquired, work to implement the system can begin. In order to implement the system, a plan similar to the curriculum development system should be prepared. Either the latticing technique or a similar modeling technique can be used to plan the implementation steps. The goal of this plan is a fully operational curriculum development system. The objectives could include staffing, staff training, securing a work environment, remodeling that environment, installing equipment, acquiring supplies, testing material, and organizing curriculum developers.

For the most part, the postmanagement tasks involve managing the business of curriculum development, that is, the curriculum development system. Here, a number of tools and techniques can be used. Some are very sophisticated. For purposes of this chapter, only two key management tools will be discussed.

Scheduling Curriculum Development Work. Once the curriculum development system is set up, scheduling can begin. Note that scheduling can begin on a tentative basis before the system is even implemented to determine ball park deadlines.

The scheduling process involves integration, sequencing, and time-lining of personnel and resources to divide products by a certain time and at a certain quality. This is done by identifying the available personnel and resources and allocating them to each subtask identified in the implementation plan.

Personnel can be assigned to various subtasks, and the subtasks can be made a part of their job descriptions. Supervisory staff can be assigned work on the basis of the more encompassing objectives. Supervisory staff and development staff will be directly responsible for their subtasks and objectives. These tasks and objectives should be included in each person's job description and used in evaluating their performance.

The plan for the curriculum development system can also be used as the basis for staff orientation and training. Objectives and tasks provide an orientation to more detailed work. Procedures within tasks can be used as the content of staff training. Such training can minimize the effect of turnover and provide staff with the skills and understanding required to do each job.

Once tasks and objectives are assigned, tables of organization can be completed. It should be noted, however, that tables of organization can only be used to illustrate who is responsible to whom. The real game plan is the schedule.

There are a number of scheduling techniques, including the Critical Path Method (CPM) and the Program Evaluation and Review Technique (PERT). Both CPM and PERT are too sophisticated for most curriculum development systems. Probably the most widely used scheduling tool is the Gantt chart, developed by Henry Gantt during the nineteenth century.

Figure 5 is such a Gantt chart. This chart illustrates what is to be done, who is to do it, and when it is to be done. Gantt charts can be made more sophisticated with the addition of percentages of time and detailed tasks.

Basically, a curriculum development schedule (like Figure 5) is developed by putting the objectives, subobjectives, tasks, subtasks, and procedures in a column down the left side of the sheet. Only objectives and supervisory staff have been included in this sample schedule. In a real schedule, all staff and their assigned subtasks would appear. The next column contains the names of the persons responsible for each task. The remaining columns identify the period of time in which tasks are to be accomplished.

With staff input, a management team can develop time projections for each objective and task. Time projections should be equalized to the extent possible so that no particular person is over- or under-utilized. This process is called balancing. After the balancing is finished, the schedule is complete.

Why is the curriculum development schedule such a key management tool? A high-quality schedule has these key benefits: It serves as a roadmap that tells staff and management what should be done and when. It serves as an evaluation tool to determine whether objectives are being met on time and whether there is a smooth work flow and to pinpoint problems and make adjustments. Finally, it serves as a mechanism for communicating the work that is to be done, how well it is being done, and what may be preventing it from being done.

The Individual Workplan. The manager cannot do all the work by himself. The staff is the backbone of the curriculum development system. Each person must do a good job and do it on time. If someone lags behind, this impedes the work of others and affects the outcome of product development.

Each staff member should be evaluated for his or her individual contribution to the team effort. If someone is not performing to a set standard, action must be taken. The first action would be to help the person to meet the performance standard. The final action would be to relocate or terminate the person who either cannot or will not meet performance standards.

The manager becomes the link that oversees the performance within the curriculum development system. Budde (1979, p. 188) states: "To manage performance in human services effectively, a human service manager must (1) be committed to managing performance, (2) collect and use objective data, (3) evaluate performance

Figure 5. Curriculum Development Schedule

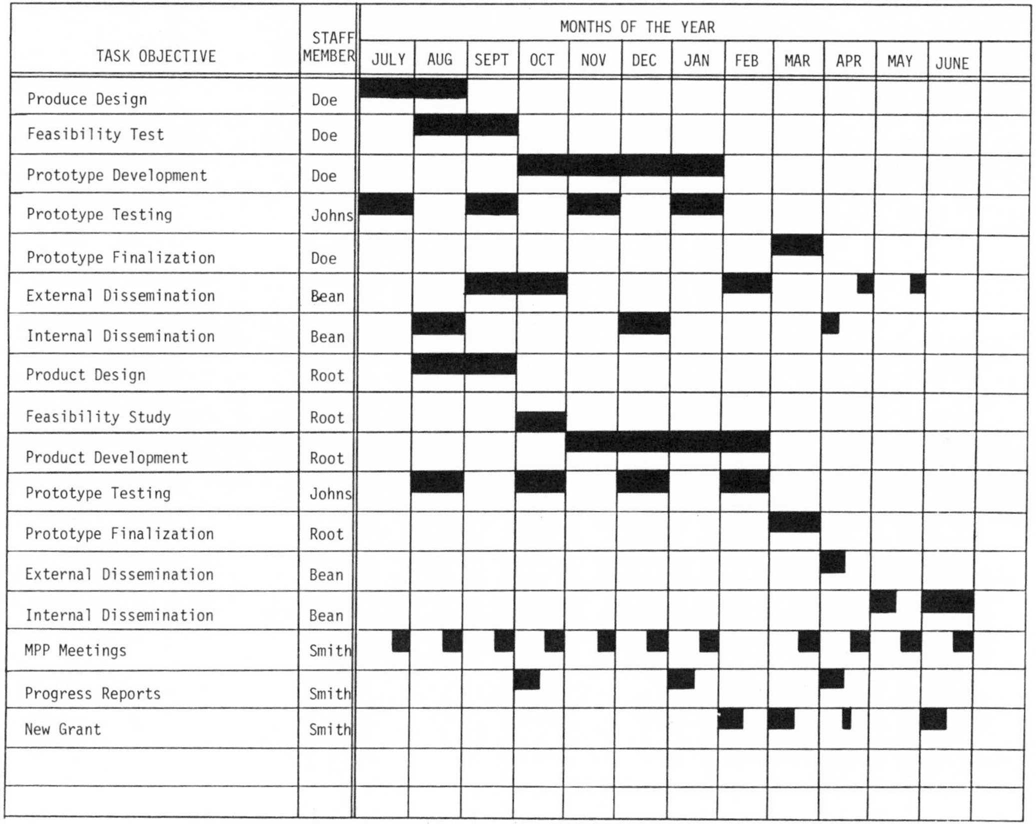

MONTHS OF THE YEAR

TASK OBJECTIVE	STAFF MEMBER	JULY	AUG	SEPT	OCT	NOV	DEC	JAN	FEB	MAR	APR	MAY	JUNE
Produce Design	Doe												
Feasibility Test	Doe												
Prototype Development	Doe												
Prototype Testing	Johns												
Prototype Finalization	Doe												
External Dissemination	Bean												
Internal Dissemination	Bean												
Product Design	Root												
Feasibility Study	Root												
Product Development	Root												
Prototype Testing	Johns												
Prototype Finalization	Root												
External Dissemination	Bean												
Internal Dissemination	Bean												
MPP Meetings	Smith												
Progress Reports	Smith												
New Grant	Smith												

systematically, and (4) be willing to provide monetary increases or other reinforcers or terminate staff on the basis of performance. He cannot ignore any of those areas; for to do so would be to weaken the contingency link."

The term *performance standards* is used in manufacturing, but it is also highly applicable to the business of managing curriculum development. Performance standards can be developed merely by estimating the number of tasks that an employee will do and integrating them into a work plan. The work plan can then serve as a performance evaluation and feedback tool.

Figure 6 is an example of an individual work plan or Management Program Plan (MPP). It is somewhat similar to the Gantt chart. Objectives or tasks are listed down the left side, and months are listed across the top. The major difference between the MPP and the Gantt chart is that each task or objective contains a performance standard for each month; for example *conduct twenty task analyses*, *test ten content areas.*

Each month, performance data are collected and compared with the performance standard. Both the actual data and the percentage of performance are specified. At the end of a certain period of time, averages are computed.

The MPP can be used in several ways. Performance can be assessed daily. Day-to-day adjustments can be made to determine whether monthly performance standards will be met. Intermediate assessments should be made monthly. Temporary monthly adjustments can be made as necessary. Formal and long-term assessments and recommendations should be made every six months or each year.

Quality evaluation of products and subproducts should be built into the curriculum development system and performed at predetermined intervals. The quality of the curriculum product reflects the quality of a person's work. Peer review, supervisory evaluation, and product testing can all be used to evaluate quality. If quality standards are not met, the product or the task should not be counted as completed on the MPP. In this way, quality deficits will show up on the MPP.

The MPP is not the only type of evaluation that is needed, but it is probably the critical one. Other evaluations should concern the quality of work, personal traits, work habits, and job skills.

It is quite possible for a person to be a high performer but possess undesirable personal traits. Persons with undesirable traits

Figure 6. Example of a Management Program Plan

NAME: Mary Sommers

DATE: 1-1-80 - 5-30-80

RECOMMENDATIONS:

1. Salary merit increase recommended at 78 percent.

2. Job should be modified to increase control development and testing load and decrease task analysis load.

	JAN		FEB		MAR		APR		MAY		JUNE		AVERAGE	
	#	%	#	%	#	%	#	%	#	%	#	%	#	%
Conduct 20 task analyses	15	75	10	50	15	75	20	100	10	50	25	125	15.8	50
Develop 10 content areas	7	70	8	80	11	110	9	90	9	90	12	120	9.3	93
Test 10 content areas (5 in May, 5 in June)									5	100	4	80	9	90
Overall Average												78		

can make the environment unpleasant and affect the performance of other staff. Numerous assessment procedures and remedies that deal with each of these problems can be found in the management literature.

MPPs can be used effectively in both evaluation and feedback to control and improve the system. They can help to get at other problems that are directly related to performance. They can be used as a contract, particularly when salary increases or other reinforcers are used in conjunction with them. The MPP is a visual representation of the history of an individual employee. It serves as a permanent record, and it can be used to settle grievances. It also provides data for the writing of progress and final reports.

Conclusion

In this chapter, the author has described approaches and tools that can be used to manage a curriculum development system. There are many other useful concepts, principles, procedures, and tools. The author hopes that this introduction will serve to confirm the good work and ideas of curriculum development managers and to create some new ideas.

References

Budde, J. F. *Measuring Performance in Human Services.* New York: AMACOM, American Management Association, 1979.

Mayer, W. V. (Ed.). *Planning Curriculum Development: With Examples from Projects for the Mentally Retarded.* Boulder, Colo.: Biological Sciences Curriculum Study, 1975.

Silverman, L. C. "Systems Engineering for Education." In *Quantitative Concepts for Educational Systems.* Los Angeles: Education and Training Consultants, 1972.

James F. Budde is director of the Research and Training Center on Independent Living, Kansas University, Lawrence.

*A procedure for testing and teaching reasoning skills is
described based on test data collected from several groups of
mentally retarded students. These are summarized, and
directions of current validation procedures are outlined.*

Curriculum-Directed Research: Assessment of Problem Solving Based on an Inductive Teaching Strategy

I. Leon Smith
Sandra Greenberg

This chapter describes a series of investigations into development of a procedure for assessing the problem-solving skills of mentally handicapped (MH) learners. The underlying assessment model was derived from an instructional theory about facilitation of social competence and adaptation (Goldstein, 1974a, 1975a, 1975b, 1976; Goldstein and Goldstein, 1980). One important feature of this theory is that facilitators or teachers should make systematic use of an inductive teaching and problem-solving strategy. This strategy is characterized by a

The authors wish to thank Nick Falcone and Jessica M. Smith for their technical expertise and Ruthanne Bessman and Deborah Harkness for their assistance in preparing the manuscript.

H. Goldstein (Ed.). *New Directions for Exceptional Children: Curriculum Development for Exceptional Children*, no. 6.
San Francisco: Jossey-Bass, June 1981

unified organizational theme: systematic movement of the learner through successive stages of awareness, beginning with identification of a problem and its parts and ending with the production of rules for solving an entire class of similar problems. The flow of classroom events can be conceptualized as a vertical spiral that moves from a point where a problem is unrecognized to a point where the problem is defined, hypotheses are generated and tested, and generalizations are produced and applied.

The teacher employs a highly structured five-step sequence to enhance and facilitate the vertical spiral progress of learners toward the ultimate goal, rule governed behavior. These five steps have been named *labeling, detailing, inferring, predicting-verifying,* and *generalizing.* In the early stages, the teacher helps students to gather and examine information relevant to the problem. The next stages require the learner to use the relevant facts to produce potential solutions and to determine the adequacy of these solutions. The final stages require students to develop a generalizable rule; that is, a rule that is applicable both to the problem under consideration and to other, related problems.

The inductive teaching strategy is part of a larger instructional theory about facilitation of general social competence and adaptation among MH learners. In the larger theory, social competence is defined as a function of critical thinking and independent action. Critical thinking involves the ability to use a store of social facts and concepts (content knowledge) within a systematic problem-solving framework (process knowledge) in order to generate solutions and rule-governing behavior. Likewise, independent action is related to an individual's ability to act on the outcomes of critical thinking and to adjust behavior accordingly (content and process utilization). With respect to critical thinking, the inductive teaching strategy delivers content knowledge and demonstrates a systematic problem-solving process. With respect to independent action, the active participation required of the learner by the inductive teaching strategy enables the learner to use both content and process knowledge in the class-room and provides practice for decision making in the real world.

Research has shown that classroom use of the inductive teaching strategy facilitates the adaptation skills of MH learners (Schimoler and Warshow, 1978). A wide variety of tested instructional materials that use the inductive teaching model is available. These materials can help to improve the productive thinking and social inference behavior of MH learners (Goldstein, 1972, 1974b, 1975c; Goldstein, Mischio, and Minskoff, 1969; Mayer, 1974; Ross and Ross, 1972; Rouse, 1965; Selman, 1980; Spivak, Platt, and Shure, 1976; Spivak and Shure, 1974; Tisdall, 1962). To summarize, the inductive teaching strategy is designed specifically for use with MH learners. It consists of a highly structured sequence, consistent with the literature on hierarchial learning models (Bloom, 1956; Gagné, 1968; Gagné and Paradise, 1961; Hill and McGaw, 1981; Kropp, Stoker, and Bashaw, 1966; Madaus, Woods, and Nuttall, 1973; White, 1973), that constitutes a more elaborate and detailed version of the inductive, discovery, and scientific methods of teaching (Keislar and Shulman, 1966; Smart, 1972; Strike, 1975; Wittrock, 1966) that have been utilized with nonhandicapped learners (Joyce and Weil, 1972; Taba, Levine, and Elzey, 1964).

Rationale for Assessing the Problem-Solving Skills of MH Learners

Examining Assumptions Underlying the Inductive Strategy

One reason for assessing the inductive problem-solving skills of MH learners is to examine specific assumptions based on the instructional theory. One assumption is that the steps are so ordered that an individual's ability to respond at one step is prerequisite to the individual's ability to respond to the next step within the same sequence. A second assumption holds that, owing to the developmental nature of the critical thinking processes, each step or process can have a threshold age below which performance is less than adequate.

Both assumptions are directly related to the process knowledge element in critical thinking and indirectly related to the social content knowledge element in critical thinking. However, both content and process elements are linked, because the instruction materials provide not only social facts but also the vehicle through which process knowledge is transmitted. Problem solving is not taught in a vacuum; rather, it is linked to social adaptation concepts and facts that have both immediate and long-term value for the learner. This means that any assumption concerning the underlying aspects of process knowledge should be valid when linked to any piece of social content.

A third assumption is that the development of both critical thinking and independent action affects the display of social competency in real-life situations. Not only is there a relationship between the vertical progress of students within the inductive sequence and their ability to think critically, but there is an overriding relationship between these problem-solving processes and real outcome behavior.

Simulating Real Classroom Events

Translation of the inductive teaching strategy into a structure for assessing problem solving should provide an appropriate vehicle for experimenting with various instructional variables so that applied research affecting the implementation of the teaching methodology can be designed and conducted. Simulated classroom events could help to determine how well the methodology works with different types of teachers and different experimental conditions. For example, it is known that inductive behaviors are hierarchically acquired; this implies a general instructional sequence, but it does not specify how the behaviors should be taught. So, even if we know that labeling behaviors should be acquired first, does this mean that a teacher should focus exclusively on this level to the exclusion of all others? What are appropriate and reasonable distances between the levels at which students can perform and the levels at which the teacher is working? Well-designed variations in the use of the assessment procedure should permit empirical testing of hypotheses concerning these and related issues.

Evaluating Instructional Effectiveness

Another benefit of a procedure for assessing the problem-solving skills of MH learners is that it enables us to evaluate the effectiveness of instructional interventions where the inductive teaching strategy is employed. In two large-scale, federally-funded curriculum development programs, an inductive teaching strategy has been used to deliver the content of instruction to the pupils. These projects are the Biological Sciences Curriculum Study Program for Special Education and Career Awareness (Mayer, 1974) and the Social Learning Curriculum (Goldstein, 1974b, 1975c). Establishing the effectiveness of these programs requires development of valid and reliable measures of postintervention conditions. The Joint Dissemination Review Panel (JDRP), established by the Education Division of the Department of Health, Education, and Welfare to review the effectiveness of educational products and practices developed through federal funds, regards the use of valid and reliable measures as essential for adequate evaluation and subsequent endorsement by the Education Division (Tallmadge, 1977). The JDRP specifies that a valid measure has a logical relationship to what is being measured. An evaluation of elements of the Social Learning Curriculum (SLC) that follows the JDRP guidelines is currently being conducted in order to compare the effects of the SLC with another major intervention program, Instrumental Enrichment (IE), as well as with traditional special education programs (Cunningham, 1980). IE is an educational intervention program that supplements regular curriculum activities. The goal of IE is to attack deficient cognitive functions and promote development of the higher mental processes that facilitate problem solving. As described earlier, the SLC utilizes the inductive teaching strategy to promote the development of problem-solving processes underlying social competence. Since the SLC must be evaluated for its usefulness in assisting MH children to develop and use social problem-solving skills, a procedure for measuring problem solving must be employed to determine whether the program is actually achieving its stated objectives. The same measure also makes it possible to assess social problem solving in other studies of the postintervention effectiveness of programs that make use of an inductive teaching strategy or that emphasize general social problem solving skills. See Brandwein (1980) for an example of this type of study.

Assessing Social Competence

A number of measures of adaptive behavior have been developed in the last decade. The measures in current favor are the AAMD Adaptive Behavior Rating Scale (Nihira, Foster, Shellhass, and Leland, 1969, 1974), the public school version of the AAMD Adaptive Behavior Rating Scale (Lambert, Windmiller, Cole, and Figueroa, 1975), and a portion of the Mercer and Lewis (1978) System of Multicultural Pluralistic Assessment called the Adaptive Behavior Inventory for Children. While these tools differ in purpose, scope, and psychometric sophistication, they are similar in the method by which information is collected. Questions concerning various dimensions of behavior are answered by a parent or someone else with knowledge of the child. Although this type of assessment is useful for situation-specific evaluation, it does not solve the problem of assessing adaptive behavior in the broadest sense. First, there is no way of knowing all the situations in which an individual will be expected to function (Baumeister and Muma, 1975). Second, all the relevant domains of adaptive behavior cannot be included in a single instrument. Third, the measures currently available tell little about the ways in which an individual perceives and interprets the social world.

Adaptive behavior implies two different types of qualities. The first can be called *skills*, and they can be seen as behaviors. The second can be referred to as *processes*, and they can be conceptualized as the action of acquiring skills. These distinctions are consistent with what Ryle (1949) has called *know-that*, or skill competence, and *know-how*, or procedural competence. With the exception of the Test of Social Inference (Edmonson, deJung, Leland, and Leach, 1971, 1974), all measures of adaptive behavior currently available overlook procedural competence, despite the growing literature on social understanding and social cognition (Greenspan, 1980). Even the Test of Social Inference measures only one generic process, namely, the ability to generate inferences concerning social situations and cues; it does not consider either the processes involved in generation of the inferences or the processes involved in subsequent deployment of the inferences in some systematic fashion. Translation of the inductive teaching strategy into a structure for assessing problem solving should provide a more epistemologically complete assessment of the processes underlying social competence.

Coordinating Assessment and Instruction

However, psychometric sophistication has no virtue and little benefit unless it leads to some form of rational instructional intervention. In this connection, a test model based on the inductive strategy should enable assessment to dovetail with the provisions of P.L. 94-142 on the testing, classification, and placement of MH pupils. In the past, evaluation was viewed as a tool for educational placement, not as an aid for individual program planning. Today, with the array of new legislative requirements, "evaluation must be drawn from a variety of sources, results are to be analyzed and recommendations made by a team of persons rather than by an individual, and tests aimed at assessing educational need (as opposed to IQ) must be administered" (Turnbull and Turnbull, 1978, p. 95).

Traditional testing practices have penalized students from culturally diverse backgrounds, causing an undue number to be placed in special education classes (Mercer, 1973a, 1973b; Mercer and Lewis, 1978). The inductive assessment model is nondiscriminatory, because it directly presents the specific content on which the concepts are to be based.

Development of individual education programs (IEPs) is a major concern of administrators and teachers. In this connection, an inductive assessment model would dovetail with cognitively based curricula that use an inductive teaching strategy and be useful with field-tested and published programs of instruction specifically designed for educable mentally retarded (EMR) pupils (Goldstein, 1974a, 1975, 1978; Mayer, 1974).

The approach provided by the inductive assessment model seems well founded in light of the recent concern over use of norm-referenced evaluation procedures with MH students. Ysseldyke and Bagnato have stated, "norm-referenced devices have a legitimate function in providing a global picture of students' abilities, interests, and psychological attributes, but they have limited utility at the secondary level, especially for program-planning purposes" (1976, p. 283). Similarly, pointing to the obvious disadvantages of norm-referenced procedures, Haywood (1976) has called for procedures that assess behavioral and social processes and lead to development-enhancing implementation programs. The inductive assessment model and its underlying theory of social competency take the direction advocated by Haywood while at the same time providing a complete picture of problem-solving skills in our best normative-test traditions. Full interpretation of test results has three benefits: general characterization of performance, specification of process weaknesses in the hierarchy, and development of curricula designed to facilitate social adaptation.

Studies of Problem Solving Based on the Inductive Strategy

The Children's Analysis of Social Situations (CASS), an assessment procedure developed by Lehrer, Greenberg, and Melnick (1971), is amenable to all the broad applications outlined in the previous section. The CASS was adapted from the Test of Social Inference (TSI), a test designed to measure social adjustment skills of EMR adults (Edmonson, deJung, Leland, and Leach, 1970, 1974). The TSI approach focused primarily on the inference level and did not assess the other levels in the inductive problem-solving sequence. The CASS consisted of fifteen pictures of people and common objects placed in a variety of social situations. Primary and intermediate level EMR students, age six to twelve, were asked to respond to the same series of questions concerning each picture. The questioning sequence asked children to state what was happening in the picture, what could have produced the situation, how the situation could be resolved, and a rule for solving either the problem shown in the picture or a class of problems comparable to the one depicted.

Examination of the data focused on assumptions related to the process knowledge aspect of critical thinking—ordering among the scored levels and the developmental nature of these levels (Smith and Greenberg, 1973; Greenberg and Smith, 1974). Results on the ordering of levels were generally consistent with the predicted model, but one major break in the presumed linear ordering of levels was noted, so it was not possible to trace performance at the generalization level to a systematic combination of performance at all the other levels.

Within the age levels examined, the ability to perform on the inductive levels appeared to follow a developmental pattern. The youngest subjects, six- and seven-year-old primary level EMR students, were capable of labeling and detailing. The oldest subjects, eleven- and twelve-year-old intermediate level EMR students, were capable of making inferences and predictions. Only a few of the oldest subjects were capable of producing a response at the generalization level.

Further analyses examined the relationship between measured intelligence and the inductive problem-solving levels. Although the correlations between IQ and the levels increased from labeling through generalization, the relationships were not sufficiently strong to justify an interpretation that the inductive problem-solving process is synonymous with measured intelligence.

While the assessment procedure was not intended to provide formal strategy training, the CASS did permit two kinds of strategy learning to be examined as a microcosm of what is expected to occur in an inductively managed classroom. The assumption was that exposure to the series of fifteen picture stimuli in the CASS is similar to presentation of the content of the SLC in the classroom. The first kind of strategy learning, a *respondent-to-operant shift*, was defined as a change to a higher level of first response across the fifteen pictures in the series. For students who exhibited this pattern, the use of the entire series of pictures, each with its constant set of questions, functioned as a quasi-training program. Since the cues provided by the test administrator appeared to become less important in focusing the students' responses as time wore on, it seemed plausible to assume that these students were beginning to employ the inductive strategy independently. A second kind of strategy learning, *shift within the respondent role*, was defined as a change to a higher level of final response across the series of fifteen pictures. Students who exhibited this pattern appeared to be demonstrating strategy learning, but only in direct response to the questions in the sequence. Assessment of these two types of strategy learning is similar to what Budoff and his colleagues have referred to as "learning potential" (Budoff, 1975; Budoff and Corman, 1976; Budoff and Gottlieb, 1976).

Results of the CASS analyses confirmed the basic assumptions about critical thinking. At the same time, however, they pointed to a need for revisions in the instrument itself. The basic format—stimuli materials depicting social problems and a standard interview designed to elicit performance on levels of inductive reasoning—was retained, while the content of the stimuli materials and the interview were both revised. First, it was decided to link assessment of inductive reasoning skills with presentation of a series of stimulus cards depicting related problem situations. In that way, the interaction of social content and inductive reasoning performance could be examined. In addition, the use of multiple problem situations related to a single rule or principle allowed for more effective and realistic assessment of generalizing skills. As a result, a decision was made to develop three stimulus cards for each social problem area to be tested. The three cards represented different aspects of a single problem area and provided the subject with direct, problem-solving experience. Second, since the inductive strategy incorporates the notions of prediction and verification of potential solutions, a new type of stimulus material was developed: a set of resolution cards that depicted possible solutions for each problem. Use of the resolution cards allowed subjects to verify most of their own predictions about solving the problems. Third, major changes were made in the interview sequence designed to elicit performance on levels of inductive reasoning. Instead of assessing the entire set of inductive reasoning skills with each of the stimulus cards, the new interview sequence made assessment of the highest inductive level, generalization, contingent upon the presentation of all three content-related stimulus cards.

On a conceptual level, these modifications and extensions were made to relate the assessment of inductive reasoning skills more closely to the development of inductive reasoning as it was perceived to occur. The result was the Test of the Hierarchy of INductive Knowledge (THINK), so named to focus attention on the assessment of an ordered sequence of problem-solving processes. Figure 1 displays operational definitions of the nine levels measured by the THINK and relates them to the five steps of the inductive teaching strategy.

It should be noted that the think assesses inductive reasoning only as it emerges in response to a highly structured interview sequence. It is not a measure of inductive problem-solving perform-

Figure 1. Operational Definition of Test of the Hierarchy of INductive Knowledge (THINK) Levels and Relationship to the Inductive Teaching Strategy (ITS) Sequence

ITS Sequence THINK level	Operational Definition
Labeling Label	Name of object or individual.
Detailing Detail	Descriptive qualities of object or individual.
Inferring Visual Inference	Relationships among people, expressed emotions, placement or action, and causal events leading to the problem.
Statement of Problem	Inference concerning the nature of the unresolved conflict.
Solutions-Qualifications	Alternative hypotheses for resolution of the unresolved conflict.
Best	Solution judged to have the highest probability of solving the problem.
Predicting-Verifying Predictions-Verifications	Consequences of the alternatives and assessment of the consequences.
Generalizing Learning Statement	Conclusion concerning the problem and its solution based on a single problem card and associated resolution cards.
Generalization	Principle concerning resolution of the class of problems depicted in the theme.

ance in naturalistic, nonguided situations. Therefore, the THINK also included two independent attempts to measure the degree to which the inductive problem-solving process was utilized by the subject to solve new social problems that differ from those social problems employed to assess the process itself. The problem-solving materials included for this purpose were viewed as application tasks, since the subjects were judged on their ability to utilize process and content knowledge independently. Thus, the THINK was designed to yield two general classes of responses. Performance on the nine levels of the process itself was referred to as the *respondent mode,* because the test situation is under the control of the experimenter. Responses on the two application tasks were referred to as the *operant mode,* because the test situation is at least partially under the control of the subject.

In its final form, the THINK is an individually administered assessment device requiring subjects to respond to sets of 21.8 by 28.2 centimeter black-and-white line drawings. In the respondent mode, there are four separate sets of pictorial materials, each relating to a different social learning concept or theme: sharing, object substitution, dressing appropriately, and responsibility. Each set contains three cards depicting problem situations related to the social learning concept as well as cards representing alternative resolutions to the problem situations. In the operant mode, each set consists of one card depicting a problem situation and several resolution cards. One set deals with emergencies, the other with seeking assistance.

Administration of the THINK requires approximately fifty minutes per subject. Following a warm-up in which the task is explained, the subject is handed the first problem card from Theme 1 and told to hold it in an upright position on the desk. The accompanying resolution cards are placed face down to the subject's left. As the subject examines the card, the experimenter begins the interview sequence. When the administration of Theme 1 is completed, all material is removed from view. The remaining themes are administered in a similar fashion. The sequence for Theme 1 is typical of the THINK interview procedure for all themes in the respondent mode:

> Problem Card 1: Look carefully at this picture. Tell me every-
> thing you see in the picture.—Tell me more. Tell me
> what you see happening in the picture.—Can you tell
> me any more? How does he (she, they) feel right

now?—Why? What is his (her, their) problem? How can that be solved?—Can they solve it another way?—Any other way?

Resolution Cards: What is the very best way of solving it? [Each question card is sequentially presented after asking] How would it have worked if_____[description of the resolution]?—Were you correct?

Problem Card 1: Now I want you to think very carefully. What did he (she, they) learn today about solving the problem of _____ [statement of the problem]?

Problem Cards 2 and 3: [Interview procedure is the same as for Problem Card 1.]

Problem Cards 1, 2, and 3: [Pointing to each card as appropriate:] Now I want you to think very, very hard. You told me the things that these people learned today. This person learned _____ [appropriate learning statement], and this person learned _____ [appropriate learning statement], and this person learned _____ [appropriate learning statement]. If you were telling other children how to solve these problems, could you tell them just one thing that would help them the most? Make it a good rule that would help them solve all these problems. Remember, I want one rule that would help other children solve all of these problems.—Why is that rule important?

During the operant mode of assessment, the single problem card is handed to the subject while the accompanying resolution cards are placed face down to the subject's left. The following represents the THINK interview procedure for each task in the operant mode:

Operant Task: Do it just like all the others. Go ahead, but talk out loud.—Uh huh, go ahead.—[Accompanied by nod or glance in the direction of the resolution cards:] How about these? Is that all? Anything else?

The overall sequence of testing calls for administration of Operant Task 1 after Themes 1 and 2 and of Operant Task 2 after Themes 3 and 4.

For the sake of clarity, the discussion of results that follows is structured around six questions addressed by data collected from administration of the THINK. The complete set of results summarized here can be found elsewhere (Brandwein, 1980; Greenberg, 1977; Singer, 1975; Schimoler and Warshow, 1978; Smith, 1978, 1980a, 1980b; Smith and Greenberg, 1979, 1980, 1981; Smith and Greenberg, in preparation).

First, is performance on the levels cumulative and hierarchical from the simplest level, labeling, to the most complex, generalizing? Examination of data collected from 120 EMR students, age nine through fourteen, confirms a hierarchy among the first four levels. The first break appears at the solutions-qualifications and predictions-verifications levels, which suggests that they may be empirically more complex and possibly nonunitary processes. The second break appears at the generalization level, where the inability to demonstrate the hierarchy may be due to the complexity of the process and the age range of the sample. Very few pupils were able to perform at this level.

Second, is performance on each of the levels developmental, that is, age-related? As a result of the hierarchical organization of levels, is age also related to progress along the sequence? Do older children tend to perform better on some or all levels in the process than younger children? Examination of results concerning the age-relatedness of the THINK with primary and intermediate-level EMR students supports a linear developmental pattern across all levels. From a more qualitative perspective, the verbal responses of subjects seemed very limited beside the array of visual stimuli built into the test materials and the comprehensiveness of the interview format. The nine- to ten-year-old subjects often made responses related only to the label and detail levels. The eleven- to twelve-year-old subjects show more ability to produce inferences about the causes of the problem, but their responses were inadequate at the higher inference levels. Although these subjects produced the greatest number of solutions-qualifications, they did not always produce an adequate best solution from among the alternatives generated. The thirteen- to fourteen-year-old subjects appeared most capable of producing responses at all levels. It should be noted that even though the older subjects were most likely to respond adequately at the highest level, only 30 percent of the fourteen-year-old subjects produced appropriate generalization responses. Thus, age alone may not always indicate better social problem-solving skills, particularly among lower functioning or institutionalized populations. For example, in comparison with the total sample described earlier, the performance of a group of institutionalized adult moderately and mildly retarded individuals in a vocational program was found to be uniformly lower on all THINK levels.

Third, is performance on the THINK levels related to the more traditional estimates of adaptive behavior referred to as measures of skill competence? In order to answer this question, scores on the THINK levels were related to teacher judgments concerning the adaptability, social appropriateness of behavior, socialization skills, and ability to act reasonably, of primary and intermediate EMR pupils, who were also rated on academic competency, attitudes toward school work, involvement in group activities, and willingness to persist in efforts to attain goals. Examination of these results indicates that performance on the THINK levels is significantly related to teacher ratings. That is, the THINK levels explain approximately 20 percent of the variation on the teacher ratings, with the solutions-qualifications and predictions-verifications levels making the largest contribution.

Fourth, is performance on the THINK related to estimates of psycholinguistic ability? An examination of the correlations between two subtests of the Illinois Test of Psycholinguistic Ability (Auditory Reception and Verbal Expression) and performance on the levels of the THINK among primary and intermediate level EMR students demonstrated only minimal relationships. The nature of the interview schedule appears to account for these minimal relationships. The interview schedule allows ample time and permits positive reinforcement to encourage subjects to verbalize responses. It appears that the crediting of responses on the higher levels of the THINK is dependent not on word production or vocabulary but on the problem-solving level implied by the response.

Fifth, how many problem-solving levels are actually needed in order to describe pupil performance efficiently and adequately? Can the levels be combined empirically in order to form fewer levels? What is the relationship between the empirically reduced levels and other cognitive and stylistic variables? The data indicate that the nine THINK levels can be reduced to three factors without loss of important information concerning individual performance. One dimension appears to involve information storage and retrieval, while the other two represent information processing. The information storage and retrieval factor is best characterized by the two lower levels of labeling and detailing. The visual inference, statement of problem, and solutions-qualifications levels appear to define one information-processing factor; they symbolize behaviors associated with the overall process of exploring, mulling over, or ruminating upon the data. A second information-processing factor is best represented by the best and learning statement levels; they indicate decision-making behaviors associated with reaching a conclusion. From a practical perspective, these three factors can be conceptualized as problem finding, problem exploring, and problem resolving. A similar factor structure has been obtained from independent analyses of three samples—two primary and intermediate level, school-age EMR populations and one group of adult moderately to mildly retarded individuals in a vocational institutional setting. Independent analyses of these three samples indicate that while the problem-finding and problem-resolving factors do tend to have a slight to modest relationship with IQ, status on a standardized intelligence test does not appear to be a good indicator of the THINK processes associated with these two factors. With respect to the problem-exploring factor, intelligence test data from the three samples tell virtually nothing about this THINK dimension. Problem exploration, has, however, been found to be negatively related to age in the samples, negatively related to length of institutionalization in the vocational sample, and positively related to the dimension of reflectivity-impulsivity in the school-age EMR samples (that is, reflective children are better problem explorers than impulsive children).

Sixth, are responses to the two application tasks in the operant mode related to aspects of performance in the respondent mode? Is the level of performance demonstrated in the operant mode limited by the level attained in the respondent mode; that is, is strategy application constrained by strategy knowledge? Does a comparison of the performance on the two application tasks provide evidence that an EMR sample can learn to generate new knowledge through application of the inductive problem-solving process? Examination of the results indicates that primary and secondary level EMR students do less well in the operant mode than in the respondent mode. Based on the criterion of the highest level attained in both modes, subjects were found to produce responses approximately two levels lower on the application tasks. There was a strong linear increase in performance on all levels of the operant tasks across the entire age range, and it was comparable to the increase reported for performance on levels in the respondent mode. Older children performed better than younger children, regardless of the type of functioning assessed. Comparisons of performance on the first and second operant tasks clearly indicate that students resonded in a more sophisticated fashion on the second task. The average increase in performance was approximately one level. Further, the increment in performance appeared to be quite uniform for all age levels examined, that is, age nine through fourteen.

Current Efforts

The development of the THINK and the analyses reported in the preceding section focused on questions of validity. There was little attention to the procedure as an individual assessment technique. While it was possible to make general statements about an individual's performance on the measure, the full meaning of that performance was not explored with a broad range of individual difference variables. The work reported here was primarily directed toward construct validation of the instrument and only secondarily toward refinement of the procedure for the purposes of individual decision making. Since the evidence for construct validation of the procedure appears to be favorable, it seems appropriate now to reorient the work in a direction that continues previous construct validation efforts and adds translation and presentation of test data in a form that facilitates decision making and program planning. The results of the previous work indicate also that a broader range of individuals needs to be tested in order to explore the limits of the assessment procedure and to develop a more comprehensive and representative picture of the performance of MH individuals. A research program designed to accomplish these objectives is being now conducted under a three-year grant from the Department of Education, Office of Special Education.

Current work is focused on modification of the stimulus materials and interview procedures. The development of nondiscriminatory pictorial material to elicit performance on social problem-solving levels is a priority. Guidelines for the portrayal of ethnic and racial minorities, the aged, the handicapped, and males and females in age-appropriate, nonstereotypical roles and statuses are available (Carlton and Marco, 1980; Consortium for Appropriate Representation of Exceptional Persons in Educational Material, no date; National Retired Teachers' Association, 1979; Tittle, 1980). Test materials require further modification and evaluation in order to obtain test item specifications relevant for a wide age range of ethnically, racially, socially, and geographically diverse individuals, whose only commonality is their psychometrically documented status as MH individuals.

A pilot study is being currently conducted to identify test item bias resulting either from discriminatory portrayal of characters within the stimulus material or from inadequate representation of the social content of problems. In accordance with currently accepted test sensitivity review practices, particularly vigorous efforts are being made to represent black Americans, Hispanic Americans, and women (Hunter and Slaughter, 1980; McGraw-Hill Book Company, 1974). Judges are being asked to examine each stimulus item and to describe the sex, ethnicity, age, and affect of all characters represented. Judges are also being asked to note stereotypical representations, as well as irregularities related either to graphic portrayal of the characters or to the nature of the social problem content. These developmental efforts are being documented (Smith and Greenberg, 1981).

References

Baumeister, A., and Muma, J. "On Defining Mental Retardation." *Journal of Special Education*, 1975, *9* (3), 293–306.

Bloom, B. S. (Ed.). *Taxonomy of Educational Objectives.* Vol. I: *Cognitive Domain.* New York: McKay, 1956.

Brandwein, H. "Social Problem Solving and Vocational Rehabilitation." Unpublished doctoral dissertation, Yeshiva University, 1980.

Budoff, M. "Measuring Learning Potential: An Alternative to the Traditional Intelligence Test." In G. R. Gredler (Ed.), *Ethical and Legal Factors in the Practice of School Psychology: Proceedings of the First Annual Conference in School Psychology.* Philadelphia: Temple University Press, 1975.

Budoff, M., and Corman, L. "Effectiveness of a Learning Potential Procedure in Improving Problem-solving Skills of Retarded and Nonretarded Children." *American Journal of Mental Deficiency*, 1976, *81* (3), 260–264.

Budoff, M., and Gottlieb, J. "Special-Class EMR Children Mainstreamed: A Study of an Aptitude (Learning Potential) Treatment Interaction." *American Journal of Mental Deficiency*, 1976, *81* (1) 1–11.

Carlton, S., and Marco, G. "Methods used by Educational Testing Service Testing Programs for Detecting and Eliminating Item Bias." Paper presented at National Symposium on Educational Research, Washington, D.C., Nov. 1980.

Consortium for Appropriate Representation of Exceptional Persons in Educational Material. *Guidelines for the Representation of Exceptional Persons in Educational Material.* Columbus, Ohio: National Center on Educational Media and Materials for the Handicapped, no date.

Cunningham, J. *Evaluation and Comparison of the Social Learning Curriculum and Instrumental Enrichment.* Washington, D.C.: Office of Special Education, U.S. Department of Education, 1980.

Edmonson, B., deJung, J. E., Leland, H., and Leach, E. M. *Manual: A Test of Social Inference.* Eugene: University of Oregon, 1970.

Edmonson, B., deJung, J., Leland, H., and Leach, E. *Social Inference Training of Retarded Adolescents and the Test of Social Inference.* Eugene: University of Oregon, 1971.

Edmonson, B., deJung, J., Leland, H., and Leach, E. *The Test of Social Inference: Demographic and Validity Data, Administration and Scoring Guide.* New York: Educational Activities, 1974.

Gagné, R. M. "Learning Hierarchies." *Educational Psychologist,* 1968, *6,* 1–9.

Gagné, R. M., and Paradise, N. E. "Abilities and Learning Sets in Knowledge Acquisition." *Psychological Monographs,* 1961, *75,* (whole number 518).

Goldstein, H. "Construction of a Social Learning Curriculum." In E. Mayer, G. Vergason, and R. Whelan (Eds.), *Strategies for Teaching Exceptional Children.* Denver, Colo.: Love Publishing, 1972.

Goldstein, H. *Problem-Oriented Social Vocational Adaptation Program (POSCAP).* New York: Curriculum Research and Development Center in Mental Retardation, 1978.

Goldstein, H. "Social Learning: A Curriculum Element in the Education of Retarded Children." Unpublished manuscript, Yeshiva University, 1974a.

Goldstein, H. *The Social Learning Curriculum: Phases 1–10* Columbus, Ohio: Merrill, 1974b.

Goldstein, H. "Many New Curriculum Programs for Retarded Children Emerge." *The Centerline,* 1975a, *1,* 10.

Goldstein, H. "Importance of Social Learning." In J. M. Kauffman and J. S. Payne (Eds.), *Mental Retardation: Introduction and Personal Perspectives.* Columbus, Ohio: Merrill, 1975b.

Goldstein, H. *The Social Learning Curriculum: Phases 11–16.* Columbus, Ohio: Merrill, 1975c.

Goldstein, H. "Curriculum Design for Handicapped Students." *The High School Journal,* 1976, *59* (7), 290–301.

Goldstein, H., and Goldstein, M. T. *Reasoning Ability of Mildly Retarded Learners.* Reston, Va.: Council for Exceptional Children, 1980.

Goldstein, H., Mischio, G., and Minskoff, E. *Demonstration and Research Project in Curriculum and Methods (Final Report 32-42-1700-1700).* Washington, D.C.: Office of Education, U.S. Department of Health, Education and Welfare, 1969.

Greenberg, S. "Assessment of Inductive Problem Solving Among EMR Students." Unpublished doctoral dissertation, Yeshiva University, 1977.

Greenberg, S., and Smith, I. L. *Structural Validation of a Behavior Hierarchy Underlying an Inductive Teaching Methodology.* New York: Curriculum Research and Development Center in Mental Retardation, Yeshiva University, 1974.

Greenspan, S. "Social Intelligence in the Retarded." In N. R. Ellis (Ed.), *Handbook of Mental Deficiency: Theory and Practic.* (2nd ed.) Hillsdale, N.J.: Erlbaum, 1980.

Haywood, H. C. "Alternatives to Normative Assessment." Paper presented at fourth congress of the International Association for the Scientific Study of Mental Deficiency, Washington, D.C., August 1976.

Hill, P. W., and McGaw, B. "Testing the Simplex Assumption Underlying Bloom's Taxonomy." *American Educational Research Journal,* 1981, *18* (1), 93–101.

Hunter, R., and Slaughter, C. *ETS Test Sensitivity Review Process.* Princeton, N.J.: Educational Testing Service, 1980.

Joyce, B., and Weil, B. *Models of Teaching.* Englewood Cliffs, N.J.: Prentice-Hall, 1972.

Keislar, E., and Shulman, L. "The Problem of Discovery: Conference in Retrospect." In L. Shulman and E. Keislar (Eds.), *Learning by Discovery: A Critical Appraisal.* Chicago: University of Chicago Press, 1966.

Kropp, R. P., Stoker, H. W., and Bashaw, W. L. *The Construction and Validation of Tests of the Cognitive Processes as Described in the Taxonomy of Educational Objectives.* Tallahassee, Fla.: Institute of Human Learning and Department of Education Research and Testing, Florida State University, 1966 (ERIC ED 010 044).

Lambert, N., Windmiller, M., Cole, L., and Figueroa, R. *Manual for the Public School Version of the AAMD Adaptive Behavior Scale (1974 Revision).* Washington, D.C.: American Association on Mental Deficiency, 1975.

Lehrer, B., Greenberg, S., and Melnick, G. "Test Manual: Children's Analysis of Social Situations." Unpublished manuscript, Yeshiva University, 1971.

McGraw-Hill Book Company. *Guidelines for Equal Treatment of the Sexes in McGraw-Hill Book Company Publications.* New York: McGraw-Hill, 1974.

Madaus, G. F., Woods, E. M., and Nuttall, R. L. "A Causal Model Analysis of Bloom's Taxonomy." *American Educational Research Journal,* 1973, *10* (4), 253–262.

Mayer, E. *Me and My Environment.* Northbrook, Ill.: Hubbard Scientific Company, 1974.

Mercer, J. *Labeling the Mentally Retarded.* Berkeley: University of California Press, 1973a.

Mercer, J. "Implications of Current Assessment Procedures for Mexican American Children." *Journal of the Association of Mexican American Educators,* 1973b, *1*, 25–33.

Mercer, J., and Lewis, J. *System of Multicultural Pluralistic Assessment.* New York: Psychological Corporation, 1978.

National Retired Teachers Association. *Truth About Aging: Guidelines for Publishers.* Washington, D.C.: American Association of Retired Persons, 1979.

Nihira, K., Foster, R., Shellhass, M., and Leland, H. *Adaptive Behavior Scales: Manual.* Washington, D.C.: American Association on Mental Deficiency, 1969.

Nihira, K., Foster, R., Shellhass, M., and Leland, H. *AAMD Adaptive Behavior Scale, 1974 Revision.* Washington, D.C.: American Association on Mental Deficiency, 1974.

Ross, D. M., and Ross S. A. *An Intensive Training Curriculum for the Education of Young EMR Children: Final Report.* Washington, D.C.: Bureau of Education for the Handicapped, U.S. Office of Education, 1972.

Rouse, S. "Effects of a Training Program on the Productive Thinking of Educable Mentally Retarded Children." *American Journal of Mental Deficiency,* 1965, *69,* 666–673.

Ryle, G. *The Concept of Mind.* London: Peregrine Books, 1949.

Schimoler, G. J., and Warshow, J. P. Student-Teacher Dynamics of the Social Learning Curriculum Classroom: The SLERS and Student Measures. Unpublished monograph, Curriculum Research and Development Center in Mental Retardation, New York University, 1978.

Shulman, L. S. "Psychology and Mathematics Education." In E. G. Begle (Ed.), *Mathematics Education.* Chicago: National Society for the Study of Education, 1970.

Selman, R. *The Growth of Interpersonal Understanding: Developmental and Clinical Analysis.* New York: Academic Press, 1980.

Singer, S. "Assessment of Conceptual Tempo in Primary Level EMH Children." Unpublished doctoral dissertation, Yeshiva University, 1975.

Smart, P. *Thinking and Reasoning.* London: MacMillan Education Limited, 1972.

Smith, I. L. "Reflection-Impulsivity: Substantive, Validational, and Methodological

Considerations." Paper presented at first annual conference of the Eastern Educational Research Association, Williamsburg, Va, March 1978.

Smith, I. L. "Research in Large-Scale Curriculum Development for Mildly Retarded Children." In J. Gottlieb (Ed.), *Perspective on Handicapping Conditions*. Baltimore: University Park Press, 1980a.

Smith, I. L. *Test of the Hierarchy of Inductive Knowledge (THINK): Development of An Assessment of Social Competence*. Washington, D.C.: Office of Special Education, U.S. Department of Education, 1980b.

Smith, I. L., and Greenberg, S. "The Use of Inductive Teaching and Inductive Problem Solving in a Large-Scale Curriculum for the Educable Mentally Retarded." Paper presented at third international congress of the International Association for the Scientific Study of Mental Retardation, The Hague, September 1973.

Smith, I. L., and Greenberg, S. "Hierarchical Assessment of Social Competence." *American Journal of Mental Deficiency*, 1979, *83*, 551–555.

Smith, I. L., and Greenberg, S. "Dimensions Underlying a Hierarchically Based Assessment of Social Problem Solving." *American Journal of Mental Deficiency, 1980, 84*, 411–414.

Smith, I. L., and Greenberg, S. "Nondiscriminatory Assessment of Social Competence Among EMR Individuals." Paper presented at annual convention of the American Psychological Association, Los Angeles, August 1981.

Smith, I. L., and Greenberg, S. *Social Problem Solving and Reflection-Impulsivity Among EMH Learners*, in preparation.

Spivak, G., Platt, J., and Shure, M. *The Problem-Solving Approach to Adjustment: A Guide to Research and Intervention*. San Francisco: Jossey-Bass, 1976.

Spivak, G., and Shure, M. *Social Adjustment of Young Children: A Cognitive Approach to Solving Real-Life Problems*. San Francisco: Jossey-Bass, 1974.

Strike, K. "The Logic of Learning by Discovery." *Review of the Educational Research*, 1975, *45* (3), 461–483.

Taba, H., Levine, S., and Elzey, F. *Thinking in Elementary School Children*. Washington, D.C.: U.S. Department of Health, Education, and Welfare, 1964.

Tallmadge, G. K. *The Joint Dissimenation Review Panel Ideabook*. Washington, D.C.: U.S. Department of Health, Education, and Welfare, National Institute of Education, 1977.

Tisdall, W. "Productive Thinking in Retarded Children." *Exceptional Children*, 1962, *29*, 36041.

Tittle, C. "Judgmental Methods in Test Development." Paper presented at National Symposium on Educational Research, Washington, D.C., November 1980.

Turnbull, H., and Turnbull, A. *Free Appropriate Public Education: Law and Implementation*. Denver, Colo.: Love Publishing, 1978.

White, R. T. "Research into Learning Hierarchies." *Review of Educational Research*, 1973, *43* (3), 361–375.

Wittrock, M. C. "The Learning by Discovery Hypothesis." In L. S. Shulman and E. R. Keislar (Eds.), *Learning by Discovery: A Critical Appraisal*. Chicago: Rand McNally, 1966.

Ysseldyke, S., and Bagnato, S. "Assessment of Exceptional Students at the Secondary Level: A Pragmatic Perspective." *The High School Journal*, 1976, *59* (7), 282–289.

I. Leon Smith is vice president for Programs at the Professional Examination Service in New York City. Sandra Greenberg is an assistant professor of special education at Marymount Manhattan College in New York City.

Index

109